Books by Dean Gualco

A Nation of Businesses: Building a Business in the "Make it on your own" Generation (2021)

Take the Right Road: Finding the Right Job, Being the Right Employee, and Becoming the Right Person (2018)

Words to Live By: Quotes and Stories That Inspire Our Time on Earth (2016)

Making a Difference: Changing the World in Which You Live (2013)

The Choices and Consequences of our Age: The Disintegrating Political, Economic, and Societal Institutions of the United States (2012)

The Good Manager: A Guide to the 21ˢᵗ Century Manager (2010)

The Great People of our Time (2008)

The Meaning of Life (2005)

What Happened to the American Dream (1995)

THE
PERFECT COUNTRY

THE TRAITS AND CHARACTERISTICS OF
A GOOD AND DECENT PEOPLE

DEAN GUALCO

THE PERFECT COUNTRY
THE TRAITS AND CHARACTERISTICS OF
A GOOD AND DECENT PEOPLE

iUniverse books may be ordered through booksellers or by contacting:

iUniverse
1663 Liberty Drive
Bloomington, IN 47403
www.iuniverse.com
844-349-9409

Because of the dynamic nature of the Internet, any web addresses or links contained in this book may have changed since publication and may no longer be valid. The views expressed in this work are solely those of the author and do not necessarily reflect the views of the publisher, and the publisher hereby disclaims any responsibility for them.

Any people depicted in stock imagery provided by Getty Images are models, and such images are being used for illustrative purposes only. Certain stock imagery © Getty Images.

ISBN: 978-1-6632-5580-8 (sc)
ISBN: 978-1-6632-5581-5 (hc)
ISBN: 978-1-6632-5582-2 (e)

Library of Congress Control Number: 2023916248

Print information available on the last page.

iUniverse rev. date: 09/29/2023

we can't do everything,
but we can do something

To my children, Gunner and Tori,
who have given me a blessed life.

CONTENTS

"always look for the good along the road of life"

ACKNOWLEDGMENTS

I have long believed that if we can dream the impossible dream, be determined to achieve it, never fear failure or what other people think, work hard, do what's right, and always look for the good, then we will have greatness within our grasp. Fame and fortune are not the determining factors of a great life but rather that you fought the good fight, did the best you could with what you had, did what is right, and made a difference in some small way. It has been a great ride, and for that I have been blessed, and I am thankful to many who have helped me along my path. Some of those people are:

- The Man Upstairs: you have made this all possible.
- To Mom and Dad: few have ever done more for their children than my parents.
- My maternal grandmother, Vee McCoy, and paternal grandparents, Bocci and Rose Gualco: thanks for the solid reputation you gave me.
- Bill Munroe, John Ellis, Sierra Brucia, and Jeff Thompson: friends come and go, but there always seems to be a couple you have for life. I'm fortunate to have 4 and couldn't be more thankful.
- Finally, to Jon Smith: I knew Jon from the second grade until my freshman year of college, when he was killed by a drunk driver. He was one of the best guys I've ever met—or will ever meet. He never had the chance to live his life and reach his destiny. Jon died more than thirty years ago, and while his chance to make a difference was short-lived, this fact pushes me to make a difference with whatever time I have been granted on this earth.

...life is what we make it

INTRODUCTION

We just don't seem to like each other anymore.

In previous times, we lived and died in the same town, often working with our family, and having friends that last a lifetime. Our doors were unlocked at night, and we leisurely strolled our neighborhoods all the while seeking the conversations of those we met along our walks. We built community centers, helped travelers along their way, and donated books to the library. We joined sporting teams, swam in local pools, and played in parks. We watched Fourth of July celebrations, attended street picnics, and helped our friends at their house. We joined churches, civic clubs, and social groups, also participating in cleaning town squares and beautifying city landscapes.

Where have those days gone?

One would be challenged to find any of these endeavors today in places from New York to Los Angeles. Instead, we argue rather than debate, criticize rather than praise, and degrade rather than dignify. We rarely talk to those we know, and seldom socialize with those we do. That seems like a bygone era, a relic of a different generation or, worse still, a different country. The past may not have been idyllic, but it seemed more safe, more friendly, and more considerate.

Where did it go wrong?

Today, Republicans vilify the Democrats, and Democrats denigrate the Republications. The poor despise the rich, and the rich ostracize the poor. Organizations mistreat their employees, and employees detest organizations. Citizens shun immigrants, and immigrants scoff at citizens. It is rare for employees to socialize with their co-workers, few know their neighbors, and lasting friendships are foreign. Not in all instances, but it seems more common than uncommon – more certain than uncertain, that there will be disagreements and disengagements among people, rather than harmony and hospitality. The U.S. Congress Joint Economic Committee made a similar statement in their report titled, "Losing our Minds: Brain Drain across the United States," remaking that, "if we are connecting less with communities and people who are different than us, we could be more likely to see adversaries among those in whom we might otherwise find a neighbor." That is sad.

Can it get better? Can we do better?

Can at least some of the values that made America the country of promise and beacon of hope be reborn, or at least reconstituted? Not the values of discrimination and superiority that marked some of our history, but the values of work and thrift, consideration and compassion, and self-reliance and self-sufficiency. Does such a place even exist today? What country offers its citizens that type of life, that type of future, in lands seemingly more violent, more contentious, and more hateful than in recent history. More importantly, how can countries and their citizens build a place that is ambitious and promising, respectful and tolerant, kind and giving?

Some countries of the past, and probable countries of the future, have and will create this type of place by promoting five key traits and characteristics amongst its citizens. It may not result in the perfect country, but these traits and characteristics offer the best chance, and greatest opportunity, to create a place of goodwill and good fortune. These traits and characteristics include:

- Commonality – there are variables of this word including commoner and common, all reflective of a person or persons who have similar – in some but not all – aspects of their attitudes, perceptions, opinions, and emotions. They also have similar ethics, morals, principles, and beliefs, typically forged through parallel lives either lived in the last century or the next. It is these commonalities that connect one person to another, one group to another, and one society to another, creating a shared sense of purpose that advances the person we are, and the place we live.

- Compromise – a concept that evokes a visceral reaction from some, especially from a generation that believes in individuality not collectivism, independence not dependence, differences not sameness. People strive to be unique not similar, and this lack of conformity can have a devastating impact on nations seeking to build a society whose members think, believe and act with similar principles and ideals. But it is through the norms, customs, and cultures we create and share as a people that determine how we interact with our fellow citizens, the level of acceptance and respect we exhibit as a people, and the way we live and love as a human being. This requires, in at least some way, that we constrain our individual ambitions so that we can attain our collective aspirations.

- Contribute – the strongest countries of their day became strong because their citizens gave more than they took. Some sacrificed so that others – people they may never meet – could have a chance of something brighter, but it is the many average and ordinary citizens who produced more than they consumed, who paid more than they cost, that created an economy that benefited the many rather than the few, and a place where nearly everyone was afforded the opportunity to make it, if they only chose to dream for it, save for it, risk for it, and work for it.

- Gracious – a gracious person is one that is kind and courteous; a gracious community is one that is welcoming and charitable. A gracious place is composed of decent and honorable people pursing noble and just ambitions. Whether these ambitions are ultimately achieved is irrelevant. Simply through the pursuit of these ambitions, its people will create a citizenry of virtue and goodness; one seeking to do better and be better even amidst the stumbles and setbacks along the way.

- Gratitude – no one has it all. People who are content and serene are those who realize that others are never given something more, only something different. The cheerful and joyful are those grateful for what they have, not ungrateful for what they don't have, and then they seek to do something with what they have. The acknowledgment that everyone has something, and the realization that we must do something with what we have, creates a people who are appreciative of their gifts, and thankful for their opportunities.

It can be done. We can create a place where citizens share virtuous **common** values, where a sense of **compromise** benefits the many and not just the few, where we **contribute** our unique talents and skills to the betterment of our communities, where we are kind and **gracious** to our fellow man, and where we are **grateful** for the good fortune in our lives. These are the traits and characteristics of people searching for something better, of neighborhoods building something stronger, and countries offering something brighter.

It really can be done.

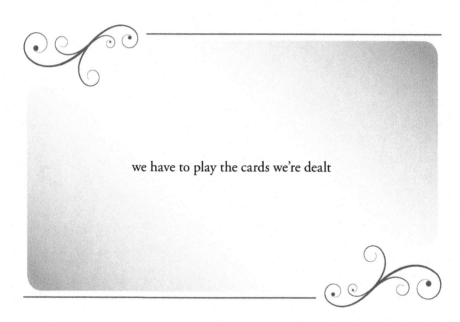

we have to play the cards we're dealt

CHAPTER 1

COMMONALITY

When we think and act identically to others, it is easy to get along. We have shared holidays, raise children in a similar manner, and worship a common God. We believe what our neighbors believe and behave as our friends behave. There is little that distinguishes one person from the next, one city from the next, and one state from the next. What does distinguish one person from the next is inconsequential, even fascinating to a degree, because we share comparable histories and seek commensurate futures. The operative words are similar and common.

Prior to, and for period after, its founding as a country, the United States was a place similar to any other on Earth. Its people had a similar history and common present. This circumstance may be a result more from the lack of transportation, communication, and technology, than from a desire for adventure and exploration. Because of the lack of ready transportation, nearly all citizens resided, worked, and died in the same plot of land on which they were born. They had the same jobs as their parents and grandparents, socialized among the same family and friends as their ancestors, and knew little of the universe beyond their small town or village. It was a simple, quaint, and peaceful existence.

Except for a few, the ability to travel far and wide was non-existent. One simply did not have the money, let alone the food or shelter, to journey beyond the narrow confines of their town, and long-distance travel was further compounded by lack of navigation, safety, and darkness. For these reasons, interactions among those within a province or state were limited, and maybe infrequent, and led to a greater degree of commonality amongst citizens than what would occur for later generations.

It was the advent of travel, and then technology, that began to change the landscape of the United States. While horses were commonplace during this period, it was the advent of the railroad by the mid-1800s in the United States (though railroads were introduced in England much earlier, beginning in the seventeenth century). While steamships allowed for the travel of individuals throughout the waterways, railroads were a completely new phenomenon. Now Americans – all later people throughout the lands – could travel at a faster, and safer, pace than ever before. This new invention, aided by investments from U.S. government, opened up the frontiers enabling people to search for employment beyond their hometown, and to seek adventure in far-flung places previously unexplored, even unheard of.

Industrial Revolution

The emergence of railroads occurred simultaneously with the rise of the Industrial Revolution. The Industrial Revolution, generally occurring between the 1750 and 1850, started in Great Britain and was the primary event that transitioned that country, and subsequently the United States, from an agrarian society to one built by industry. Iron and steel were the materials used in production now (which facilitated the emergence of railroads) and power was created by new materials from coal to steam. Manufacturing was to become the predominant source of employment and income for citizens, who were less tied to their homeplace for their livelihoods and could instead embrace a workplace away from their land and dwellings. The "commonality" that was restricted to family and a few friends, was to be expanded to those who now worked together in factories and plants.

Work transformed the home, whereas previously the home transformed work. People were able to choose where they worked and settled, not only the community but also the state or even the country. The rise in transportation facilitated the movement of people from one place to another, in addition to economic conditions in foreign lands that made it difficult for citizens to

2

remain. And they came from many towns and states. Around the 19th century, the California Gold Rush brought thousands from China, and later 5 million Germans (National Museum of American History, n.d.). About the same number of Irish came as a result of the massive famine, and another 650,000 Africans were forcibly brought to the United States in the years prior to 1860, a number that grew to the 4 million emancipated by President Abraham Lincoln by the Civil War (history.com).

Immigration played a key role in the growth of the United States. According to the census population during that time, the population of the United States grew from about 5 million to about 23 million between 1800 and 1850. The population, then, quadrupled in a scant five years. No question, there were tremendous benefits and advantages to the population growth during this time. The country was able to offer jobs, and employ millions of people in the building and construction of new industries and new communities, enabling untold numbers of people to not only aspire, but realize, more beneficial circumstances than where they came from. This was the birth of the "American Dream," a circumstance where the current generation reached a higher standard of living than the previous one, and where it was expected that the next generation would continue this ever-rising standard. It was a belief that, in these lands, that the sun would never set upon these lands, that it would be a brighter and more luminous, and that tomorrow would always be a better day.

To be sure, those born in the United States, along with the millions of immigrants, had to work for nearly any success they achieved. Few governments in any country, let alone the United States, offered welfare or unemployment assistance to its citizens, and few employers offered retirement or health care benefits to their employees. That was simply not offered or done during those times. It was a "make it on your own" adventure, with little in the way of a safety net to catch those unable or unwilling to create or sustain their own standard of living. There existed an ethos that through hard work, thrift, risk, and sacrifice (a circumstance we discuss later in this book), you could make it if you only tried; if only your interests matched your efforts. These were the values that were defined an era, even a century, whether one was born here or immigrated from other lands.

Common Values

From the 1700s through much of the 1900s, most of the population resided among people who had the same cultures, whether that be their traditions or customs. For the most part they believed in the same God and pledged allegiance to the same government. They celebrated the same days of the year and mourned the fallen in the same fashion. Save for a few countries such as the United States, this commonality was born through shared histories.

This was a time when individuals died in nearly the same town in which they were born. If you were Italian, you lived in Italy; if you were Chinese, you lived in China; and if you were Peruvian, you lived in Peru. These same histories created similar values, or at least values that were understood and followed, if not respected, mainly because these values were passed through generations of families through prairie after prairie, community after community. It was the way people were raised to act, behave, and believe; at least if we were born and lived in the same lands. It was the way things were done.

Over centuries, the United States became a place absolutely, utterly, profoundly and completely unique to any other lands. Unlike Ireland or Japan, Nigeria or New Zealand, the United States was a populace built mainly on immigration and migration, far more than nearly any other country on record, with a notable exception is the United Arab Emirates, which is composed of almost 90% immigrants (worldpopulationreivew.com, 2023). As of 2020, there were almost 45 million immigrants currently living here, or about 14% of the U. S. population. This was not the highest percentage of immigrants within the U. S. population, though: in 1890 almost 15% of the U. S. population was comprised of immigrants, an increase from 10% in 1850 (Ward & Batalova,

2023). Immigration, then, has long played a strong role in the growth of the United States.

Given this level of growth and composition of the country, especially in these recent years, a sense of camaraderie or community, is not easily obtained or sustained. In times past, there were familiar and religious pressures for children born and raised in these communities to accept the traditions and customs, and considerable public pressure for any travelers or foreigners to adopt these traditions and customs. Decades of "sameness" occurred where children followed their parents into the same home and the same occupation. Grandparents and grandchildren, in fact, often inhabited the same house and worked in the same fields, offering an often-daily reinforcement of how the young were to be raised, and how the old were to be treated. This was recorded, and glamorized, in the television show *The Waltons,* where grandparents lived with parents and children, performing the same occupations, and contributing to the family's general welcome.

In some ways it was a much simpler time and existence; in other ways, it was a confining, even limiting, existence where one's fate was pre-ordained and pre-determined, with little ability to decide on one's own destiny or choose one's own path. What were the values prevalent during those times? Advantageous or disadvantageous, positive or negative, constructive or destructive; there were several collective values that defined the United States from its founding to much of its existence. These values became part of the American experience; part of the American phenomenon that helped create the preeminent country of its time. They can be collected into five general categories – self-reliance, limited government, thrift, faith, and exploration – with each described and debated in greater detail below:

- *__Self-reliance__*. When the United States was founded, nearly all jobs centered around farming. That was to be expected: there was little science or technology to create new methods and materials required of more advanced jobs; the lack of electricity and refrigeration meant that plants and trees had to be continually farmed and harvested; and animals raised and killed in order to best assure a continual supply of food. This forced most citizens to work in agricultural; a necessity that continued through the middle 1800s.

Thus was the type of work offered, and few opportunities existed for anything more. The same for governments. Federal, state, and local governments were expected to perform limited duties and functions, allowing their people a wide degree of independence to pursue their own interests. Few benefits, if any, were offered to the populace. Unemployment insurance did not exist, nor did community health care, retirement, or welfare. This is a far cry to what people demand, and governments offer and actually provide today: in 2023, over 200 million U.S. citizens receive health care through private insurance, with another 115 million provided health coverage through Medicare and Medicaid (Himber, 2022). The word "benefit" did not exist in the 1800s as it does today in the 2000s, from sick leave to holidays, short-term disability to the Family Medical Leave Act. In the past, Americans, similar to others throughout the lands were required to provide for their own needs and wants, which reinforced the notion of self-reliance, a term used less frequently today.

Self-reliance, like self-discipline, was seen as a trait, if not THE trait, that people needed to achieve their potential. That was the message of educator and author Booker T. Washington, a man of immense character who maintains considerable influence long after his passing.

• •

Booker T Washington

The story of Booker T Washington, both truth and folklore, is a story about how people – any people – can succeed. The first African American to be honored on the U.S. postage stamp, he was born in 1856 and witnessed the horrors of slavery, and then watched African American struggle for political, economic, and societal freedom for decades after. While some believed a violent struggle was the only way to achieve sovereignty over their choices and chances, Mr. Washington believed in a different, maybe fairer, way.

Mr. Washington, who was a highly noted and regarded author and orator, believed that the destiny of people lies in their ability to achieve economic prosperity. Though he quietly supported other, more strident causes to achieve these ends, he believed that individuals needed to control their fate. These thoughts were encapsulated brilliantly by the noted author Jacqueline Moore who stated in her book titled, "Booker T Washington, W.E.B. Du Bois and the Struggle for Racial Uplift," that it was Mr. Washington who believed strongly in the thought and concept that "economic independence was most important to racial equality" (Moore, 2003).

Education was a core tenant of his belief and, not surprisingly, he became the founder and first president of Tuskegee University. According to the Tuskegee University biography of Mr. Washington, some of the lessons he learned were from Samuel Armstrong, a White man he called "the noblest, rarest human being it has ever been my privilege to meet" (Tuskegee University, n.d.) Without question, Mr. Washington established a legacy that far surpasses Mr. Armstrong, and that relationship, during a challenging time in American history, showed that somewhere and someplace there was goodness between men and women, no matter their background, beliefs, or race.

Eventually, Mr. Washington wrote more than 40 books which influenced countless others with such statements as, "one man cannot hold another man down in the ditch without remaining down in the ditch with him," and "you measure the size of the accomplishment by the obstacles you had to overcome to reach your goals." Mr. Washington is beyond comparison as a man who walks among the giants of our age, one to be studied, and unquestionably emulated.

• •

• ***Limited government***. Freedom. Liberty. These were concepts incorporated into the controlling documents of this new republic – the Articles of Confederation, the Bill of Rights, the Declaration of Independence, and the Constitution. Before its founding, those that settled in the eventual United States territory were a colony of the British Empire, subjugated to the capricious will of others, in this case kings and queens, living in the foreign lands of England. Few rights or choices were permitted or extended, and a person's home and place of work were the property of a ruler in another country. Failure to submit to these terms resulted in horrifying beatings and imprisonments, possibly even death.

The American Revolution, and the subsequent Article of Confederation, were largely in response to the tyranny and despotism of the hereditary monarchs of the past and present, manifested most prominently and starkly by the English kings and queens and their appointed representatives both in England and in the American colonies. Their power, influence, and dominance of those in the American colonies were absolute. The documents that were created during and after the American Revolution were specifically written to break with the past and extol a level of freedom and determination for the revolutionaries.

These intentions were enumerated in the limited nature of any government that was to be born and was to follow on these shores. The Bill of Rights, in particular, stated emphatically in Article 10 that the government was to be limited both in scope and power, noting that "powers not delegated to the United States by the Constitution, nor prohibited by it to the states, are reserved to the states respectively, or to the people." No longer a central government of immense control.

That, at least, was the start.

To further emphasize the constrained nature of this new government, the later Constitution established a central government whose basic tenets were that actual power was diffused among three independent branches of the central government (executive, judicial, and legislative), making it incredibly difficult for one person, or a select minority, to control or dominate another. These actions, both explicit and implicit, serve to limit the role of government. The people were reclaiming rights from the previous sovereign and ensuring that their government was cognizant of the citizen's principal role in the government, and the elected or appointed person's obligations to the country – and people – they served. Many of these concepts originated with the famed economist Adam Smith, one of the most brilliant economics minds whose philosophies are still followed today.

• •

Adam Smith

Adam Smith walks along the hallowed halls of the most influential economists in history. Born in Scotland during the 18th century, Mr. Smith went to college at the University of Glasgow at the young age of 13 and later Oxford University, emblematic of his status as a child prodigy of great intellect. In due course, his philosophies on free enterprise and capitalism laid the groundwork for the spectacular emergence of the British economy and American political systems that occur in the next century.

Private property. Profit. Competition. The invisible hand. Free markets. These were all concepts studied and later articulated by Mr. Smith in his important book, *The Wealth of Nations*. Mr. Smith believed in the notion of the "invisible hand," where people invest their money, skills, and efforts pursuing opportunities that will benefit them. Whether opening their own business, or working for another person, people are guided by self-advancement, yet in so doing they also benefit the populace. As an example, the person who opens a dressmaking business can benefit financially from the endeavor, but the public also benefits materially through the opportunity to purchase a product they most likely may not have been able to produce.

That is the essence of the "free enterprise" system, an economic system that predates Mr. Smith by many centuries, but one that he perfected through his research. Mr. Smith believed that by following one's self-interest to maximize their talents and abilities, a market will be created which is composed of a plethora of products and services of the highest quality and the most competitive price (that, at least, is the intention). Moreover, a person who chooses to work, and work hard, receives the principle share of the rewards, or consequences, of their work in this system.

Competition, here, is an important component of the free enterprise system. Through competition, the best products and services will flourish in the market, and at supply and price dictated in coordination with the producers who make the product, and the consumer who chooses to buy it. This element of competition, along with choice and the "freedom" within the "free" enterprise system, is a central reason this was chosen as the economic model of the newly founded republic that became the United States.

. . . .

The concept of a limited government still permeates through wide swaths of the United States. Though the size and scope of the U. S. government has grown in many ways to the benefit of its people, this stands in stark contrast to the founder's express and written intent of a small, powerless central government that bends to the will of the people. There remains a skepticism, even aversion, to the growing role of government from segments of the population today, one that may quite possibly continue to grow. This derives from the belief that a government possessed of considerable laws and regulations can intrude upon one's liberty and infringe upon one's freedom, limiting the options from which one can choose and the actions upon which one can pursue. The movement along the spectrum from the more limited government to the more expanded government of our country, reflects a marked change for citizens to choose their own way, to make their own path. It is a different philosophy; one where there was universal agreement in the smaller government of the past versus the larger government of the present.

- ***Thrift.*** Booker T. Washington, who believed strongly and ardently in the value of thrift, once stated that, "the surest way for blacks to gain equal social rights was to demonstrate industry, thrift, intelligence, and property" (Spellen, 2022). Thrift was a virtue of many during this age because there was little to have and thus little to waste. There was no employer or government to provide for one's livelihood in the unfortunate circumstance of an illness, early death of a provider, or

11

retirement in the later years. What one obtained had to be earned, and once earned, had to be saved.

Over time, though, the various levels of government have made thrift a less important virtue, and that is a direct result of the growing power and influence of the government itself. Consider that in the 1700s, government spending amounted to less than 2% of all spending in the United States economy; by the early 1900s, that figure had risen to 7%. But by 2022 government spending was estimated to be 37% of all spending in the United States (NTUF, 2022). Much of that spending is on transfer payments, where the government transfers money from one person to another, usually in the form of fees or taxes. Unemployment insurance, health insurance, welfare, food stamps/assistance, and social security are just some of the transfer payments that flow in, and through, the government.

These monies are a great benefit to millions of U.S. citizens, and undoubtedly advantage humanity in general, but at a cost. People are less included to fund their present and future and rely upon the government to provide an ever-growing safety net to satisfy their needs. As an example, in 2022 there were about 10% of U. S. citizens who had no savings at all, and another 37% had not saved any monies for their retirement years (Olya, 2023). There is another statistic that is even more telling: in terms of personal income, the average American receives about 22% of their total income from the government. Whereas before the 1900s the average person received no government monies, the average American now received 22 cents of every dollar they have from the government. Of that amount, the average person receives 5% of their income from Social Security and 4% from Medicare.

Without question, these are averages, with retirees consuming a greater percentage of social security and those with disabilities consuming a greater percentage of health care, but these statistics are concerning, even alarming, for the population as a whole (Congressional Research Service, 2023). If someone receives money, then someone must pay money.

These are examples of a dramatic reversal in personal responsibilities from relying upon oneself for their own standard of living and increasingly relying on the government, and of those who pay an increasing amount into the government. If, and when, an unexpected event happens (a job loss or health crisis), or when an expected event occurs (for example, a retirement), more citizens are relying on others, primarily the government, for their subsistence. This rise in dependency and fall of independence, results in a more expansive government, one that may – over time – compromise a person's freedom. This unquestionably stands in contrast to the more limited government at the center of the newly created United States of the late 1700s.

- *__Faith.__* Consistent with most countries at the time, the belief in a "higher power" was a foundational element of the United States. This nation's founders, along with most citizens of the day, believed that faith in someone better, or at least something better, was one principle underpinning the growth and stability of a country. In fact, most documents forming the United States as a republic referenced religion and its impact on the populace. Consider the following:

  o The Declaration of Independence includes several references to religion and faith, including "the Supreme Judge of the world" and the statement attesting to the "protection of divine Providence."

  o The United States Constitution, in Article VII, includes the statement, "in the year of the Lord."

o   The currency states, "In God we Trust."

o   While resting their hand on a Bible, the president of the United States includes the words "so help me God" at the conclusion of their oath of office though, interestingly, that is a later addition to the oath as first promised by George Washington. It is believed that Chester Arthur was the first president to use those words in his inauguration, more than a century after the first inauguration by President Washington (Vile, 2020).

That said, however, the United States was not founded as a Christian nation, nor with national religion its citizens were required to adopt and follow. There was a clear and convincing separation of "church and state," where religion and/or a deity would control the actions of elected or appointed officials. There was, however, a belief that religious principles would guide the thoughts, actions, and behaviors of those who not only served this nation but resided within it. George Washington, in his farewell address to the nation after his second term as its president, said the following:

> "reason and experience both forbid us to expect that National morality can prevail in exclusion of religious principle" (georgewashington, 1797).

President Washington believed that religious principles were a formative element of a nation's morality. As morality dictates the good and bad behavior of a people, relying – at least in part and to a degree – upon religion and the values and virtues they promote to guide a person and nation's morality (and ethical conduct) which can be a factor in the creation of a noble and decent people. Consider the following values and virtues common in most religions, including the three religions (Christianity, Islam, and Hinduism) with the highest population of devotees:

- o <u>Honesty</u>. The belief in truth, which can be further defined as a statement or action that is based on fact and/or reality.
- o <u>Love</u>. Often referred to as devotion or fondness; it is a genuine affection for another person or persons.
- o <u>Charity</u>. Compassion and sympathy are components of charity, which rests upon the benevolence of those who have some, or much, to help those who have little, or nothing.
- o <u>Forgiveness</u>. Forgiveness is more than pardon or mercy; it is about recognizing the fallibility of the common man and understanding that mistakes (no matter their level of intentionality) are inherent in the growth and development of a person. Forgiveness allows a person and humankind to "move on" and "move forward," enabling the mistakes of yesterday to be the lessons of today, creating a more tolerant people.

Religion is not the sole factor in creating a good and decent society, to be sure. History is littered with actions or deeds taken under the flag of religion, or by a religious people, that have had destructive ends. The crusades come to mind and, most definitely, slavery and subjugation through history. Few can understand, and no one can justify, those catastrophic events and times. This may be a continuing reason why religion as a political and societal force has weakened over the last few decades, especially within the United States. The results are indisputably evident, as noted in the following:

- o According to the Pew Research Center, in the early 1990s about 90% of the population considered themselves religious to a certain degree. By 2020 that figure had fallen to 64% (Pew Research Center, 2022).

o   In 2020, 47% of the United States stated they belonged to some type of religious organization, which is down considerably from 70% in 2000 (Jones 2021).

o   From 1972 to 2018, the share of adults who reported attending religious services once a month or more dropped from 57% to 42% (United States Congress, (2019).

o   From the 1990s to 2020, Americans who were not affiliated with any religion at all has quadrupled, from 8% in 1998 to 30% (Cohen 2022; Jones, 2021).

It is a stunning collapse of once-powerful societal institutions that, at one time, were a controlling force in the way and manner Americans lived. And it is troubling for a wide variety of reasons. For example, according to Putman and Campbell (2014), those who attend services tend to be "happier, healthier, and better spouses and parents and are more likely to engage in pro-social and community-building activities…and have levels of volunteering, charitable giving, and participation in voluntary organizations than Americans who are less religiously involved." And while religion has created or perpetuated some injustices in history, it has also been used effectively and inspirationally by individuals to address and overcome some of these very same injustices, in many cases using the values and virtues of religion as their guide. One such person was Harriet Tubman.

• •

Harriet Tubman
the "Moses of Her People"

Harriet Tubman is a seminal figure in American history. Considered the first African American woman to serve in the military, she was among the foremost individuals who helped those born into, and living through, the scourge of slavery (Michals, 2015). Through the underground railroad, Ms. Tubman shepherded hundreds, if not thousands, of indentured and enslaved black people from the South to the North. She was fond of saying that as a conductor of the underground railroad she "never ran my train off the track and never lost a passenger." Few, if any, other conductors could make that claim.

Her birth did not indicate such greatness would soon be experienced by her people. She was born into a large family in Maryland and, like most of her contemporaries, could not read or write. But during these harrowing times, her belief in freedom and justice, and her courage to pursue it, was evident. As a young girl she refused to stop a fellow slave from leaving the plantation, causing her to be beaten with a heavy weight. As a result, she suffered throughout her life with severe headaches and seizures but was undaunted in her pursuits.

Ms. Tubman's accomplishments have not only marked the times when she lived, but have stood the test of time. Even in the depths of human misery, through the most perilous of times, there was a person who became a shining beacon for others to follow, both literally and figuratively. That was Harriet Tubman. And while she may have lost faith in some of her fellow men, she never lost faith in her God, who served as her shining beacon to never give in and never give up.

"God's time is always near.
He set the North Star in the heavens;
He gave me the strength in my limbs;
He meant I should be free."

• •

17

- <u>Adventure and Exploration.</u> Their names are the lore of myth: Magellan, who acted by behalf of his benefactor King Charles I of Spain, founded the "Strait of Magellan" and even named the Pacific Ocean. Amelia Earhart was the first woman to fly solo across the Atlantic Ocean. There was Marco Polo, who traveled from Europe to China and back again. Marco may be seen as a daring explorer, to be sure, but his travels became the stuff of legend largely as a result of the stories encapsulated in the book *The Travels of Marco Polo,* which inspired legions of whom, including a certain Christopher Columbus, are often seen as great discovers of their time.

The United States is an interesting phenomenon. It was not created through an ever-increasing birthrate, but largely through immigration from foreign lands. This is reflected in the citizens of the United States rarely giving their ethnicity as American but rather as Italian or Chinese, or more frequently as Italian-American or Chinese-American. Their citizenship may be the United States, but their ethnicity (their place of origin) rarely is. They immigrated here because it was a nation founded by explorers seeking to explore for and about themselves, often to seek the attainment of what became known as the "American Dream."

The "American Dream" refers to a constantly rising standard of living, a belief that our station in life will be more prosperous than our parents, and our children's standard of living will be even greater. No other country, in memory, refers to its possibilities for its citizens to pursue as a "French Dream" or the "Peruvian Dream," mainly because few countries experienced the level of growth – economic and otherwise – as the United States over the past few centuries. This growth is not projected to continue at a similar and even constant rate in the coming century or even decades, but few can deny that the opportunities that one was presented with upon arriving in the United States were decidedly foreign in most other lands.

But one must do something with what they have been presented, or given, upon arriving in this country. In these lands, it mattered little where we were born, the family that we came from, or the title that we acquired in the years after our birth. We were as unconcerned about the privileged as the non-privileged, maybe because so many living during this time were non-privileged. It is one reason why, when George Washington was first elected president, he refused the titles of "Your Excellency" and "Your Highness." The title of "Mr. President" would be just fine, which referred more about his position that his people elected him to, rather than an inherited or acquired role or title (National Park Service, n.d.)

Life in most, if not all, instances centers around doing something with what we have, making the most of what we were given. And in many cases over the past centuries, the most opportune place for that to come true has been the United States.

Quite possibly because of the seemingly unlimited land available to citizens following the founding of the United States, there was a belief that through exploration a person could stake their own claim. A sense of adventure permeated through many of the citizens during this time, encouraging some to venture West, to explore the frontiers of land not yet inhabited, of states not yet named. They traveled by horse and buggy, and later by railroad, seeking a different way, one that offered more and greater possibilities than existed in their previous states and former countries. The amount of land appeared limitless, and so too were the dreams and aspirations.

For most of this existence, success seemed within the grasp of almost anyone, and almost everywhere. Without debate, limitations existed, but a sense of exploration and adventure remained foremost in the culture and traditions of this country. One sterling example of this belief and conviction, and faith in its possibility, was exhibited by Madam CJ Walker.

● ●

Madame CJ Walker
The First Millionaire

Sarah Breedlove was the first child born (in 1867!) in her family as a free person; her preceding siblings were all born to enslaved parents in Louisiana. From those humble beginnings she eventually married and assumed the name CJ Walker, a name history records with many firsts, quite possibly the most prominent being that she became the first female African American millionaire in history (Dunlop, 2021).

As with many during that time, it was a difficult childhood. Both her parents died before she reached adulthood, causing her to move in with her older sister. For the next several years she took a series of odd and uninspiring jobs, but then a medical condition changed her trajectory along with countless others in her path. Ms. Walker experienced significant hair loss, a fairly common occurrence because poor diets made hair brittle, and the limited indoor plumbing made hair washing infrequent (History, 2023). But she was undaunted in inventing a cure for this ailment, leading her to develop a line of hair care products for African American women that not only addressed hair loss but also led hair to become soft and even luxurious.

Ms. Walker was more than an explorer. She became one of the foremost inventors of her age. Wealth was a consequence, to be sure, but more important is what she did with it. She employed, at one point, over 40,000 employees, and then donated untold thousands to the National Association for the Advancement of Colored People (NAACP) and the Young Men's Christian Association (YMCA). She advanced the status and positions of more than herself. She created companies and industries, but most importantly she created hope. Hope in what this country offered its citizens, no matter what they have or where they start. Everyone, anywhere, could improve upon their station in life. That, more than her wealth, is the lesson we are most thankful, and most grateful, to have learned from the fascinating person we call CJ Walker.

"I am a woman who came from the cotton fields of the South. I was promoted from there to the washtub. Then I was promoted to the cook kitchen, and from there I promoted myself into the business of manufacturing hair goods and preparations."

Madam C. J. Walker
National Negro Business League in Chicago, 1912

● ●

There are, no doubt, other values and virtues that represent the United States, some from its origin and others acquired as the country matured through the centuries. For instance, education was hardly a priority during the late 1700s, not only in the United States but throughout the globe. Few young adults finished high school until the 20th century. In fact, few finished grammar school until the 20th century either. There are many reasons for the lack of interest in an educational system. Technology was primitive and therefore not much to learn through schooling. Professions were limited too, with most becoming farmers and machinists. Only as countries entered the 20th century did technology require more advanced knowledge and skills (from medicine to law, engineering to communications) that were learned in a more advanced educational system.

Today, the United States largely dominates advanced education, at least in the colleges and universities although, through an odd circumstance and twist of fate, now finds itself falling behind most of the more advanced countries in terms of primary and secondary schooling standards.

Another virtue missing from the young United States, of greater importance today, was an involvement in world affairs. In fact, the opposite was true. The United States followed a largely isolationist foreign policy, rarely becoming involved in foreign affairs unless there was a clear and present danger to the people, or borders, of the United States. In fact, the United States was one of the last remaining major powers to enter World War I and did not enter World War II until more than two years after the other global powers were engaged in battle. Even then, the United States did not enter World War II until it was attacked suddenly, and quite ruthlessly, by Japan at Pearl Harbor, Hawaii.

By the end of World War II, the United States foreign policy changed drastically. A few short years after the United States became involved in the Korean War, and then a decade later was the principal foreign power involved in the Vietnam War. The United States had moved from an isolationist posture in foreign affairs to becoming a dominant force, and a controlling player, in global political affairs. As the 20th century moved towards its close, the United States was often seen as the planet's policeman, entering various conflicts when the rule of law needed to be upheld, or a principle was seen as just to fight for. From the invasion of Grenada and Afghanistan to the bombings of Serbia and Somalia. the United States' political and military policy is so expansive, and so invasive, that as of 2022 there were tens of thousands of service members stationed throughout the lands, including Japan, Germany, South Korea, Italy, and Afghanistan.

In total, there are more than 750 United States bases in over 80 countries, totaling nearly 180,000 troops (Hussein & Haddad, 2021). Almost every country has some type of U.S. troops stationed within it, a far cry from the isolationist policy that marked the United States upon its founding. The expectation, at least, is that the United States is a safer place following this change of policy, or possibly the new world simply demands countries become involved in the political, economic, military, and social affairs of others, maybe because of the prevalence of communications, telecommunications, military hardware and software, and travel has made our spaces more interconnected and interrelated.

Ironically, patriotism is another virtue that is prominent today yet nearly non-existent when the country was founded. There was not a resounding chorus of approval for the original colonies to join into a federation of states committed to a common purpose. Common values and ideals among its people, yes, but not towards becoming a singular country beholden to a powerful government similar to England. For instance, the smaller states were suspicious of the economic and political power of the larger states. This is one reason one house of Congress, the Representatives, allocated votes according to a state's population whereas the other house of Congress, the Senate, allocated votes equally to each state in the confederation. There was also, as discussed earlier, a suspicion among the general public of nearly any form of government, from monarchy to democracy. For these reasons, there was less of a belief in the "state" and more of a belief in the "person."

This sense of patriotism is a recent phenomenon. The separatist movement that culminated in the Civil War occurred nearly a century after this nation's founding, indicative of the lack of progress made for its citizens to coalesce around central governmental principles beyond the desire for a limited government. Some of the government's more substantive advancements shortly after the ending of the Civil War can be seen as precursors to a more patriotic nation. For instance, the growth of the military and creation of universal taxes led to a powerful and controlling government, in addition to the formation of an elementary and secondary educational system. Further wars, including World War I and World War II, cemented this growing sense of patriotism, the "rallying around the flag", that has come to be a defining characteristic of the latter-day United States.

Education, global engagement, and patriotism were three virtues that arose over the century of this country's growth. The last, and far more formidable virtue that has come to define the United States, has been the recognition and appreciation that diversity and inclusion are fundamental characteristics of a good and decent place. This virtue, too, can often be seen as ironic. This republic was founded upon the principle that "all men are created equal," a statement that takes a place of prominence in the Declaration of Independence as written by Thomas Jefferson. George Washington, in his farewell address to the nation in 1796 promoted the ideal of "brotherly affection" and that the administration of the government be steeped in "wisdom and virtue" (Bill of Rights Institute, 1796). These two individuals, Jefferson and Washington, were only two of the many who espoused the virtues of freedom and fairness yet subjected many of those in their fellow human race to reprehensible human conditions and treatment, namely slavery.

Yet the United States was far from founded on the concept of freedom among people.

The United States has a complicated history related to fairness and equality. Truly there is nothing complicated about treating people in an inhuman and inhumane manner. It was simply, uncomplicatedly wrong, inconceivable, and incomprehensible. Historians and scholars have researched extensively to assess why a people believed these reprehensible thoughts and actions were right and just, but few answers have arisen. Money, greed, and self-interest were unquestionably components of this philosophy (Human Rights Careers, n.d.). For example, in the United States slavery offered not only a ready workforce to till the fields, but an inexpensive one as well. Money, greed, and self-interest, though, were not original to the United States' intention to subjugate certain people into servitude.

For nearly 400 years there were numerous European countries that enslaved swaths of people to further their economic interests. Portugal, Spain, and England were but a handful of those countries. The true origins of slavery, though, began largely with the start of civilization. Almost 7000 years BC (Before Christ) the first city of Mesopotamia arose, and those leaders bound their enemies in slavery. About 3000 years later Egypt used slaves for some of its work (a fact found among temple walls). More than 3000 years after that, England entered the fray with the Anglo-Saxons enslaving the native Britons following their invasion (Freetheslaves, n.d.). In nearly every time and period of history, one people enslaved another for their advantage and benefit.

Historically, the presence and practice of subjugation was sadly commonplace. Many instances of suppression came from controlling their own citizens or through invasion, where one country conquered another, with the conqueror enslaving the conquered. In the United States, both occurred. The new settlers dominated one race (the American Indians) and enslaved another race (the African Americans). Then also victimized one gender (women) and mistreated a host of others including the disabled, homosexuals, etc. Again, the central question is why, one that is remains challenging to answer and even more challenging to understand.

The United States, as created, was supposed to be different. It recognized that all were created equal. It believed that a basic sense of freedom and fairness was fundamental to a newly created people. Yet the conceptual framework, so articulately presented throughout the Declaration of Independence and the Bill of Rights, was not consistent with its practice. The history of the past, and the culture of the time, bound the United States to follow the practice of

25

so many other countries. In reality, the United States was not different, and was not unique – all people were not created equal.

What is confounding is how people are so revolutionary, and so enlightened, in some areas of humanity yet also so vicious and horrific in others. The answer may never be known. But what is interesting is that these same people taught the next generation to do better, and to be better. All too slowly, over time, we now live in the most progressive era in history. Where centuries ago some inhabitants were terrifyingly violent, and decades ago some people were appallingly racist, today those numbers are far fewer, and most people are far better.

Progress has been made, albeit in terms of centuries rather than decades or years, undeniably too slow and too late for those in the past. Yet, the progress of recent years has been unprecedented. Here are but two examples: in just one decade, the United States legalized gay marriage and elected an African American president. Then eight years after that, the first African American and Asian woman was elected vice-president of the United States. In nearly every aspect, the shackles of the past have been removed and almost everyone can pursue their passion, to find their happiness. They must dream for it and work for it, of course, but this is a country that still affords almost anyone the chance to make it, if they only pursue that change with a singular focus and deduction, unswayed and unmoved by whatever barriers may arise or burden that must be assumed.

Summary

The United States, as with most countries, was created with the best of intentions. At the forefront of this creation was a belief in a set of values and virtues that created, maintained, and promoted a sense of commonality among its people. Without question, establishing a sense of commonality is easier when citizens possess the same histories, thoughts, beliefs, and perspectives. Most, in the early United States, were of the same race, religion, and creed, and they also had largely the same attitudes and opinions, morals and principles.

These backgrounds, along with perspectives, were best represented in the core values of self-reliance, limited government, thrift, faith, and a sense of adventure and exploration in industry and science. Additional values were adopted over the centuries, including the advantages of an educated populace, involvement in global affairs, patriotism in one's home, and a focus on fairness and equality. Together these core values created a sense of pride and purpose in the collective nature of people living and inhabiting the same land.

To some, the United States that resides on the continent of America may seem like a divided or divisive place, whether that be politically or societally, economically or environmentally. Yet it is the presence of certain and specific core values that bind this country and its people toward a shared adventure, a shared destiny. It is not a perfect place, nor an entirely laudable one, but these values offer the promise that it could be. A sense of commonality amongst people is a component of nearly any friendship, family, and workplace, and it is upon that footing that rests many other traits and characteristics that create and sustain a good place to live too, with one of those characteristics being that people believe in the act of acceptance, and the art of compromise. It is that trait of compromise that we now turn our attention to in the next chapter.

... trouble follows the sinner,
blessings follow the righteous.

Proverbs 13:21

CHAPTER 2

COMPROMISE

Compromise. Business needs it. Friendship requires it. Marriage demands it. Politics wants it. Compromise is becoming an elusive, even foreign, word in the United States and in other parts of the globe. All too common, though, people are separated into, and judged against, as rich or poor, conservative or liberal, educated or not-educated, Democrat or Republican, female or male, or citizen or immigrant. While a degree of commonality among its citizens may be the basis for a country to thrive, or even survive, throughout the ages it is the art and science of compromise that has become a fundamental tool for inhabitants to utilize to create boundaries and bonds amongst people. It is not, as some have believed, a factor to be avoided, but instead one that must be embraced.

What is compromise? It is not accommodation, conciliation, cooperation, negotiation, and bargaining. None of those, however, capture the notion and importance of compromise. Rather compromise can best be summarized by three words: acknowledgment, understanding, and respect. Let's start the discussion with acknowledgment. At the root of compromise is the acknowledgment that there exists a differing point of view, that people see and interpret circumstances and events through entirely different prisms. Other than death and taxes, as the familiar refrain goes, there is not much that is readily agreed upon by the populace. So differing viewpoints are not uncommon or uncertain; it is a fact of human existence and interaction, and a consequence of communication. Search far and wide and wide, few would wholeheartedly agree with some if not all our opinions and stances. Therefore, compromise begins with this understanding.

An acknowledgment that differing views exist is followed by an understanding of differing views. In essence, this is where we learn about other opposing views, opinions, stances, beliefs, and ideas. It is amazing how little effort is extended towards understanding one's point of view, whether that view is meritorious or not. If acknowledging a different view is challenging, seeking to understand an opposing view has become nearly impossible for several reasons, including:

1. There is declining or little faith in institutions that were once seen as credible and respectful sources of knowledge, including teachers, political institutions, religious organizations, the media, law enforcement, and the justice system. As an example, only 16% of the populace had confidence in the print media in 2022, down from 21% in the year prior. Even worse, only 7% of people had confidence in the United States Congress, a figure that has fallen almost 50% just in the past year (Jones, 2022).

2. The belief in our truth, not necessarily the truth. While we may be entitled to our own interpretations, an interpretation is not the truth. As Ryan Martins recently stated, "the truth is universal, unchanging, proven by evidence, and cannot be owned. If 'the truth' becomes personal it loses authority" (Martins, 2020). That is one reason compromise is so challenging today.

3. We are increasingly becoming an isolated society, segmented into associating only with those who think, act, and believe as we do. One statistic is particularly telling: in his outstanding book titled *Why We're Polarized*, Ezra Klein stated that in a 25-year period between 1990 and 2020 "the percentage of voters who reside in a district where almost everyone thinks like them politically went from 1 in 20 to 1 in 5." In essence, Americans increasingly only want to live amongst those who believe, at least politically, the same as they do.

Wishfully, after acknowledgment and understanding comes respect. Respect is not always reverence or praise. At its most simplistic form, respect is acceptance. In this case, it is the acceptance that others have the right to have differing opinions, including those that may defy truth, logic, and even imagination. Though a person's influence may be diminished by facts or a more intelligent argument, they do have the right to believe what they believe.

The ability to acknowledge that different views exist, and then seek to understand why they exist in an unbiased and comprehensive manner, are necessary steps to find some common ground with those we may not agree with. The ability to respect those whose views may not be seen as well-founded, well-grounded, and well-reasoned is a challenge, but in a society where there is freedom of expression, religion, and a host of other rights, it is the price to pay for living in a free society.

Freedom, we have learned, exists because people not only have a right to express their own opinions but a duty. It does not mean they are right, or their opinions should be given weight, but there should be an acknowledgment in their ability to express them, and a respect in the institutions that allow them to do so.

Regrettably, compromise has become a more foreign endeavor in the central institutions of this country – in politics, the economy, and in our society – and it is in those institutions that the notion of compromise must be reborn, and recreated, to create a wiser and freer people. And of those institutions, it is in the political and economic realms that offer the greatest challenges and opportunities to reach compromise. We now explore both, and their impact and effect, further.

Politics

Politics has assumed a dominating role in the American populace over the past few decades. Historically, as in most countries, politics has been a mainstay of American society, but not in the consuming and passionate manner that pervades a wide swath of the populace today. When the United States was founded, the attention was less in fighting each other and more in fighting the British. And we continued to fight the British after the revolution. Thirty years after the revolutionary war we again fought the British in the War of 1812, and later that century the Spanish in 1898. Between those wars there was another war within the states, the Civil War, but most of the political fights in the first centuries were concerned with issues and concerns beyond United States borders. That continued well into the 1900s as we again focused our efforts on foreign enemies and entanglements, with World War I and World War II being amongst the bloodiest battles ever to be seen in history. As the century reached the 1950s there was the Korean War followed shortly thereafter with the Vietnam conflict. All were terribly consequential in the political affairs of a country that believed in a more isolationist policy of engagement, and continued through the later parts of the century and into the next with the Gulf Wars and the invasion of Afghanistan.

While politics was central to our people, it did not command the attention and consuming passions of the populace. We may have voted in greater percentages, but once the election campaigns were over, life returned to some sense of normality, with the vitriol and rancor fading from memory. This occurred because politics was a smaller enterprise in most arenas – there were fewer government entities (education, for instance, was not required until the early 1900s), fewer worked in government, and fewer served in government. All these agencies were less politicized a century ago. Labor and political unions, though positive in many aspects, were formed to represent employees against their employers, a complexity that added to the polarization of the workplace.

Within government itself, there were fewer efforts to influence governmental actions. Lobbyists were scarce, mainly because governments were so small that there was little money to lobby for or against. Laws and court cases were fewer in number, not only from a criminal perspective but from civil and regulatory ones as well. In all, the government offered fewer rewards to those within the industry and professions, and as a result it was not a consuming focus of the populace until later in the 1900s.

The dramatic rise in government in the mid-to-late 1900s was a catalyst to its growing importance and influence. Here are several examples:

- In 2020, about 24 million people worked for some form of government, a total of nearly 15% of total U. S. employment (Hill, 2020).

- Combining all levels of government expenditures, about 37% of the U. S. economy is driven by government spending, a figure that has more than tripled since 1910 (Trading Economics, 2023a).

- In terms of federal government spending, about 65% of spending, or 83% of all tax receipts, is centered around "transfer payments," or taking monies from one citizen and giving them to another (House Budget Committee, 2023).

  These payments are most often in the form of social security, health care, or welfare. Some of these monies were paid into the government in terms of Social Security and Medicare contributions, but the monies paid in have been insufficient to pay the monies expended, and there are many other social programs where no monies were paid into the system such as Aid to Dependent Families and various types of food stamps.

This extraordinary growth of government means that nearly all are now impacted by the consequences of government decisions, a far cry from a time in American history when it was reported that Cornelius Vanderbilt had more money than the U. S. Treasury (that was an outstanding feat for an individual). Obviously, when there are more rewards, when there is more money in the decision, there is more to fight for, and that is one reason compromise seems to be far less common. There is too much to win, too much to lose, too much to fight for, and too much to fight against.

Then came the 1990s.

• •

President Bill Clinton

William Jefferson Clinton is, and remains, one of the most enigmatic figures in political history, His humble beginning would not portend such a divisive figure. He was raised by a working single mother and a devoted grandmother. He never knew his father, and his last name actually comes from his stepfather, who was to become the central male figure in his life. While not necessarily poor, material comforts were nearly non-existent, a common occurrence in the state of Arkansas at the time.

President Clinton, though, was a gifted man. He was smart, even brilliant, and had a confidence within himself and his abilities that exceeded the available avenues to success for a person of his background. But he was driven, persevered through Harvard and Yale, and eventually became Attorney General for Arkansas. He later served as their governor for a decade, honing a set of political skills unsurpassed by many in his era. He was a talent.

He ran against, and beat, a sitting U. S. president in the 1992 election, and thereafter powerful forces on the "right" of the political spectrum sought to bring him down. Fortunately for the right, then-President Clinton made a number of missteps, including lying during a federal deposition. He was impeached by the House, then acquitted by the Senate, but the stage was set: one side, through any means necessary and available, was determined to destroy the other.

Since his term, Presidents Bush, Obama, Trump, and Biden have witnessed and encountered the same treatment, either verbally or through legislative action. The result, sadly, has been the same: the denigration and demeaning of the federal government, one devoid of respect and allegiance, to a political process that was intended to fulfill the dreams of the people they serve.

This became more prominent, ironically, during the presidency of a man who hailed from the town of Hope itself, in the state of Arkansas, by the name of Bill Clinton.

> "there is nothing wrong with America
> that cannot be cured by what is right with America."
>
> President William Jefferson Clinton
> Inaugural Address, January 20, 1993

· ·

As governments have moved from dictatorships to democracies over the past centuries, the intention was that people would have more control over what is to come. No longer would they be confined or constrained by the will and whims of unelected leaders, but rather wise and informed individuals would be selected to debate and then devise laws that would offer opportunity for those that sought it, and hope for those that needed it. That aspiration, it seems, has long passed. One side rarely talks to the other, and even seemingly wise laws are passed more by which person, or which party, proposes the law. The other party rarely wants to give the other a "win" with the realization that the "win" could cost them the next election, no matter how worthwhile or beneficial the law is. That is a shame.

Even more regrettable is the way and manner politicians interact with one another. One would have to search throughout the galaxy, it seems, before a Republican and Democrat politician are seen sharing a meal, let alone enjoying a conversation. Another example of why compromise has become a rarity in the political sphere. More than a rarity, it is nearly non-existent. Laws proposed by one party are opposed by the other for no other reason than it may benefit the proposing party during the next election. This is one reason a law is seen as "bipartisan" if only one or two members of the opposing party support it. Rarely are laws passed because they benefit the populace; often they are passed because they benefit a small segment of the populace, a segment that belongs to, and supports, the ruling party.

Cooperate? Concede? Words rarely uttered, even thought about, in the political arena. Instead, the more common words are liar and fraud, disrespectful and dishonorable. It matters little what party or ideology one espouses, it is ridiculed and derided by the other. The best of ideas is dismissed by the worst of motives.

What is particularly unfortunate about the conduct within the political system is its impact on the populace. School-aged children witness the divisive and corrosive conduct amongst our elected "leaders" and believe they can adopt the same conduct. Those in industry view the duplicity and selfishness and feel vindicated in acting in a similar fashion. The destruction of the political system – not only through an inability or unwillingness to comprise, but through the unethical and immoral conduct of some of its participants – has had a detrimental (even catastrophic) impact on its people.

Can it be saved? In an era of diminishing resources and increasing expectations, optimism is bleak. But through the art of compromise, a system viewed as dishonest, even crooked, can once again be a vehicle that propels its citizens to greater heights. To do so we need to consider, and address, the following:

- The voters. It is naive to blame the actors, and the system, within politics for what ills a country...any country. Politics, no matter the era or place, is a business. Those in politics realize if they do not produce – if they do not represent those who have voted them into office – they will be quickly replaced by those that do. This means that politicians are quite aware of who elected them, and make every effort to ensure their legislative votes meet their expectations. What voters demand, then, is what their representatives deliver. So, it is voters, in truth and practice, who are as responsible for a system that delivers for some, but not many. The rich, the unions, the aged, the farmers, the poor, and the businesses are among those who use their influence to gain from the system, at the expense of those with more limited means and resources.

However, it is still the vote that is the great equalizer, no matter the money spent, or the advertisements watched. In the end this system depends on an informed and wise voter. It is the ballot box that scores across the globe have sought access to, and it is the ballot box that has transformed the fortunes of country after country. Yet at some point, the allure of the ballot box seems to fade as citizens become jaded, even disinterested. Disinterested in the state, maybe, but not disinterested in what they can gain from the system. Like the politicians who game the system, some voters seek to do the same. This is what becomes of democracy, it seems, over time.

For any substantive and substantial change to occur in politics – for its actors collaborate and compromise for the advancement and betterment of others – it is the voter that must vote.

"remember, democracy never lasts long.
It soon wastes, exhausts, and murders itself.
There never was a democracy yet, that did not commit suicide."

Second U. S. President John Adams
in a letter to tenth U. S. President John Taylor
December 17, 1814

• <u>The actors</u>. President John F. Kennedy wrote a landmark book titled *Profiles in Courage*. Winner of the Pulitzer Prize for Literature. The book chronicled decisions made by a select number of politicians that changed the course of history, but at a price. There were chapters on Daniel Webster, Sam Houston, Lucius Lamar, and Robert A. Taft, to name a few. Each of those presented in the book was faced with a decision of great importance, one that involved choosing what was "right" versus what was politically advantageous. These individuals displayed a level of morality and courage rarely seen amongst those in the political arena. If these traits were so common in politics, so believed President Kennedy, there would have been no need to write the book. Thus, his book was meant to inspire current and subsequent generations to make the right decision, and to bear any burden that may result from their actions.

Can you imagine the legislation that could be passed if the political actors of the day displayed the principled courage represented in *Profiles in Courage?* What if decisions benefitted the deserving rather than the influential, or actions determined advanced the voters rather than the voted? What if respect and civility became the defining traits of those in the profession, and those traits subsequently viewed by a public that voted for those in into office? What if compromise became the rule rather than the exception? Then, just maybe, taxes would be more fairly paid (not only by the wealthy), the federal debt would be more efficiently and effectively managed, roads and bridges rebuilt, and the environment saved.

. . . .

The Last of his Kind

"if what you have done yesterday still looks big to you,
you haven't done much today."
President Mikhail Gorbachev

The true test of political courage is to give up almost everything – from prestige to material possessions to a powerful position – because we believe our state deserved better. Mikhail Gorbachev became the chairman of the Communist Party, effectively its president, when Russia still maintained a dominating role in global affairs. Next to U. S. President Ronald Reagan, he was a commanding figure on the international stage, heading a country with the world's second-greatest military and one of amazing geography (there are 11 time zones!). It was a place of rich traditions yet also possessing a terrifying and feared reputation.

But on assuming the chairmanship, Gorbachev inherited a place with a quest for military superiority which diverted scarce resources toward the military instead of the economy. Over time, the result was an economy that could not build homes or produce toothbrushes, where laws were unjust, the government was corrupt, public health services were abysmal, alcoholism rates were high, and a decreasing life expectancy occurred (Talbott, 2022). Communism had collapsed the economy, and he foresaw the catastrophe that was imminent. He could, like some of his predecessors and contemporaries, rule with an iron fist and continue the subjugation of his people in an effort to maintain his power at home and influence abroad. But he did not.

Instead, he became a reformer, a maverick, and destroyer of the status quo, and the dreamer of an innovative experiment. He wanted to maintain the political authority of the Community Party but liberalize nearly every other facet of Soviet existence, culminating in his people having the ability to vote. The intention was admirable, but the planning and execution were haphazard and disjointed. In the short 5 years of his chairmanship and subsequent presidency, the country previously known as the Soviet Union ceased to exist, replaced by one named Russia, along with a host of independent countries freed of the tyranny of the previous Soviet rule.

One man changed those 11 time zones and remade the political landscape. The accolades were generous and continuous, from being named *Time Magazine's* Man of the Decade to being awarded the Nobel Peace Prize. But there was also a price to pay. He was, and still is, seen as the man who ended the influence of the Soviet Union and tarnished its reputation. When he ran for president years after he first resigned, he could only garner one half of one percent of the votes cast. His actions have cost him his position and power, even his reputation at home. But he was right – he was willing to sacrifice all with the hope that he could have a chance of something different. That was quite a man.

"my life's work has been accomplished.
I did all that I could."
President Mikhail Gorbachev

• •

Is it possible? President Kennedy wrote his book because he felt those in the profession had lost their way. He wanted to encourage his compatriots to make decisions that were different, and that were wiser. He believed it was possible then. The simple, and entirely obtainable, traits of respect and civility, of courage and unselfishness, amongst the actors in this drama that we call politics could transform that industry and this country, and begin the long, challenging, and arduous journey to rebuild this courage. And it is politics and its members that should lead the way, which was the intent of the representative democracy envisioned by the founders when the country was created almost 250 years ago. It is possible.

- <u>The media.</u> There is no shortage of those to blame for a broken political system. Voters for sure, and politicians too. Another participant in politics deserving of some blame is the media. The media is increasingly seen as biased, even untruthful, and dishonest. The result is a stunning fall from grace of an industry that once had a controlling influence over its public. They were once so powerful they goaded the nation into war (the Spanish-American War) and toppled presidents (President Johnson following Vietnam; President Nixon following Watergate). Those days seem over.

The media have lost the respect and admiration of an increasing percentage of their audience. Consider the following:

  o In a recent study by the Pew Research Center, U. S. daily newspaper circulation has dropped from about 60 million in the early 1970s to about 24 million in 2020. This occurred even though the U. S. population increased from about 200 million to 330 million during this same period (Pew Research Center, 2020).

  o Employment in U. S. newsrooms has fallen almost 30% between 2008 and 2020 (Aratani, 2022).

  o In the 2016 election for president, the Media Research Center reported that coverage of then-candidate Donald Trump was 91% negative on major broadcast networks (Harper, 2020). Whether you are a Republican or Democrat, you do hope there is some balance, and some fairness, in the media coverage of our elections.

It was not always that way. Undoubtedly the media had an interest in investigating and reporting, and those stories that involved bribery or corruption amongst the highest levels of society attracted a wider audience (and more readers and viewers). But there was a level of fairness and honesty in the industry – at least in the major publications and television networks – that is increasingly rare. Television offers one example. When founded in the 1950s, television news was seen as a service provided by the network to its viewers with little expectation that profits would result. Profits were made in other areas of television. That changed in the 1980s as money flowed into networks when they developed morning news programs that attracted a growing share of viewers, which attracted advertisers to pay increasingly higher rates to reach that audience. Then cable appeared, with round-the-clock news stations attracting another growing audience. Corporations saw the profit potential in owning media entitle, and in the ensuing years General Electric bought NBC, Disney purchased ABC, and Viacom/Paramount bought CBS.

General Electric, Disney and Viacom were not only media companies, but diversified companies that believed, through their shareholders, that every segment of their business be profitable. The noble service of a news division ceased, replaced by an endless quest to attract viewers, which raised ratings and then advertising rates. With the rise of social media, the pressure became even more pronounced. No longer were network and cable news programs affording the time to investigate news stories. The need to constantly promote "breaking news" – at times with inadequate research involving dubious sources – further eroded the confidence the public had in the news, both in its investigation and reporting. Even the once venerable *60 Minutes* is no longer required viewing on Sunday night, and is no longer a staple of the top-ranked programs on television.

Some in the media have lost their way, consumed with a search for profits and a search for a customer. Once "their" customer was found, whether they be Republican or Democrat, conservative or liberal, the networks catered to the expectations and demands of that customer, not the story, or even the truth. No longer does the network or news program dictate what its viewer will watch – the viewer dictates what the network will showcase, otherwise the viewer will find another channel, or more likely, turn to social media. Already, almost 50% of the American public obtains its news from some type of social media, from Facebook to Instagram to Twitter (Walker & Matsa, 2021).

Quite possibly, more than any other factor that has caused the fall of the media, is their bias. True, whether in television or print, the media has long been biased toward the Democratic party, or liberal, political persuasion. The *New York Times,* for instance, has not endorsed a Republican candidate for president since 1956! (Laslo, 2020). Other major newspapers have a similar record (not surprisingly, not one major newspaper endorsed Donald Trump for president in 2016, though he won decisively). Decades ago, there was a greater belief – real or imagined – of balance, even fairness, in the media. There were efforts to tell the story, from both perspectives, and let the reader decide their opinion (even if the media gently hinted at which conclusion the reader should reach). Today, however, the media increasingly lead with the conclusion of an event, then detail the facts that support the conclusion promoted with scant effort to tell the other side, or at least another perspective that should be considered.

CNN and *MSNBC,* along with *Washington Post* and *The New York Times,* have a definitive slant. Those who watch or read those media outlets are usually classified as Democrat and/or liberal. Conversely, *Fox News* and *The Wall Street Journal* increasingly appeal to the more Republican and conservative segments of society. This is sad because we, as a consumer and a people, now rarely watch the same news programs. Just as media outlets are increasingly unwilling to compromise their journalistic standards to offer a more balanced view of an issue, viewers are not willing compromise on the news viewed. We seek those programs that reinforce our own beliefs. No wonder we are polarized as a place and as a people.

Once seen as a noble profession, politics has devolved into an arena composed of dishonest individuals more interested in pursuing their own self-interest rather than the broader interests of the human race they serve. One hopes that wise and learned individuals will recognize the folly and foolishness in the behaviors and conduct of those within the political and governmental halls, and instead acknowledge differences exist, seek to understand opposing views and viewpoints, and then respect the decision of others. Given the influence of government in our lives this may not address all the ills of the system and its participants, however, it is a worthy start and welcome example for others to witness and, optimistically, follow.

a good government offers…
opportunity for those that seek it,
and hope for those that need it

Economics

There are many "issues of our time." The environment is one – there is grave concern about various countries use and abuse of its environment. Racism has become another, one more widely and broadly discussed than at any time in our history. Surely since the 1960s, and discussed in greater detail throughout this book. Politics, as we have seen, has become a far more polarizing institution not just the United States but in Europe, as seen in the move towards the breakup of Great Britain and Europe (also known as Brexit) and the rise of the nationalistic spirit in the European countries of France and Germany. And then there is money.

Money has become another divisive issue, causing resentment and jealousy, envy and hate. There appears to be little compromise between those who have it, those who don't, and those who want it. Those who have money are seen as greedy and narcissistic, the cheaters and schemers. Those who do not have money are seen as lazy and irresponsible, the takers and shirkers. Both perceptions are uninformed and misguided and, more importantly, damaging to mankind.

In the movie *Wall Street,* the fictional character Gordon Gekko stated that "greed is good." He believed that through the pursuit of greed, a person would seek to advance their position or status, and that would monetarily advance humanity. Through the pursuit and acquisition of money a person could create markets and industries, benefitting a host of suppliers and employees, towns and countries. That, at least, is the concept, and there is greater truth in that statement and belief than some would care to concede.

We read earlier about one of the founders of capitalism, Adam Smith, who advanced the model which remains the economic underpinning of the United States financial system (and a host of other countries). This is the economic model that is used to decide how money is created and distributed, but it is not the only model. There are several models to choose from. There is communism, where the government owns all factors of production – money, property, goods, and services – which are produced, and shared equally among the citizens of that country. The "state," or government, controls what we do for a living, where we work, what we produce, and what we will receive. Ideally, the state is a benevolent entity and works to equally share the consequences of the land's production, or output, amongst the totality of its people. Russia (and the previously known country of the Soviet Union) and China are prominent examples of communist states.

Another model is socialism, a system where the state does not typically own the "inputs" but determines the "outputs." A citizen has some, or greater, choice to decide what they want to do; whether that be a farmer or doctor, electrician or painter. However, the consequences of their work (in terms of income, property, goods, etc.) are shared more equally among the people. Citizens may choose to study for 10 years to become a doctor or work 12-14 hours a day to start and manage a business, only to see the results of their labor and the rewards of their efforts, go to a person who chooses to drop-out of high school and play video games day after day. Thus, in a socialist system there is little motivation to improve ourselves because any rewards we receive for doing so go to everyone, including those who have not done so.

Socialism, like communism, relies on citizens to work, invest, and sacrifice equally, so that all rewards are shared equally. No civilization in history has ever produced such a citizenry, one reason why socialism and communism have always failed as an economic system – those that made it resent paying for those that have not. Over time, this system drains an economy not only of money but enterprise as well, as those who pay resent those who take, while those who take expect those who pay to continually do so. The fallacy of these systems is, as former British prime minister Margaret Thatcher once said, "the problem with socialism is that you eventually run out of other people's money" to spend (Perry, 2020).

Finally, there is capitalism. Here, citizens pursue their own talents and motivations to become who they want and to pursue what they want, and they get to keep (most) of the consequences of their talents and motivations. With some limited involvement and restrictions imposed by the government, citizens can keep the astounding monetary gains of their talents and motivations or, in some cases, keep nothing because their talents and motivations did not work, or were not valued by the populace. In either case, we choose our journey, make our path, and determine our destiny.

In reality, it is basic human theory. History shows that when people value something, and keep what they work for, they will pursue it with greater aspirations and motivations. Shortly before World War II, former British prime minister Winston Churchill stated that "by every device from the stick to the carrot, the emaciated Austrian donkey is made to pull the Nazi barrow up an ever-steepening hill." (Clements, 2006), The Bible and other religious books, too, recognized the importance of the carrot-and-stick motivational philosophy, inferring that "if you... then He will." Genesis 1 states that "first darkness than light" while Jeremiah 1:4-10 writes "his word to the nation is first judgment than salvation." (Glen 2013). Centuries of literature and thought have shown what is encapsulated in capitalistic economics: allow people to keep what they want (rewards), and they will exert nearly every effort, and overcome nearly any punishment.

The United States, as we know, did not invent capitalism. From an economic model, as early as the 14th century countries encouraged their citizens to farm their lands and keep the spoils of their efforts. England in the 18th century, we have read, continued to build on the capitalistic system of economics. But it was the United States that perfected it, though not without controversy. Some believe there are other models that offer greater promise, and less peril, than capitalism and point to the examples offered by those countries in the Nordic region of the global. That conversation is intriguing, yet misguided, as discussed below:

• •

The Nordic Countries

The best economic system history has produced is capitalism. It has lifted millions from poverty, afforded millions more with unforeseen opportunities, and benefitted countless others whose age or physical/mental capabilities limited their abilities to provide for their present or their future. Others, though, see another economic system as superior, that practiced by the countries of the Nordic regions of the Earth, including Denmark, Finland, Norway, and Sweden.

In actuality, the Nordic "model" is a hybrid of many systems, promoting a high degree of social welfare (pensions, income distribution), high taxes (46% in Denmark and 40% in Norway) coupled with some aspect of free-market capitalism (Kenton, 2020; Kenton-2; 2021). While the US has some social welfare, its taxes are considerably lower at 24% and there is far greater freedom within its economics markets.

It is true that the Nordic model has greater economic equality. But its GNP grows at a much slower rate than the US. It is also true that the Nordic populations are happier, but they have advantages that the US does not encounter: a citizenry with the same histories and traditions, universal agreements on political issues, and limited immigration (McWhinney, 2022). The US, on the other hand, has the most diverse population base of any place which, while societally rich and fascinating, leads to more division political and a lack of commonality societally (Bhattacharyya, 2022).

Which is more productive? Economically, the US model outperforms just about every known system in existence. But societally and politically, the Nordic models create a happier and more harmonious culture. So which would one prefer? That debate depends on your perspective along with one's definition of "better."

• •

It is unfortunate that an economic system that has advanced nations so greatly, from providing a plethora of social services to opportunities to countless others, is seen by even a few as the cause of inequality and inequity. In fact, it is just the opposite. CNBC, a left-leaning media giant, published a study that only 8.5% of the world's rich inherited their money; almost 70% were self-made and a further 23% had a combination of inherited and self-created monies (Clifford, 2019). Thus, the vast majority of those that "made it" made it on their own, and it is through the economic system of capitalism that a vast majority of these people "made it." Maybe, at some time and some place, the politicians and socialists who use the distribution of money as a tool to divide the populace will be fair and honest about the cause of inequity and inequality. And rather than misrepresenting and misstating capitalism, they will realize it is the vehicle that has afforded nearly anyone, in any place, with the opportunity and the chance to achieve something in the times in which they live.

Summary

In the century after the United States was founded, there was a sense of faith in government and in society, though there were instances of struggles and disagreements (civil rights comes to mind, as does the Civil War). Most believed in the worth of their government, their churches, their courts, their media, and their fellow man. But these institutions played a small role in the affairs of man, mainly because most had little to rely upon other than their own efforts and the support of their family and some friends. By the early 1900s, that began to change, especially for the government.

Social Security, aimed and providing income to the old and disabled, was passed in 1935. By 2023 there were 71 million citizens receiving some type of support under this system (Research, Statistics and Policy Analysis, 2023). Medicare, directed towards providing medical insurance and services to those who cannot afford it, has over 65 million enrolled in the program (Medicare Advocacy, 2022). Another 41 million receive food stamps each month (Center on Budget and Policy Priorities, 2022). To pay for these benefits taxes have increased greatly: income taxes were first passed in 1913 at a rate of 1% for the richest of citizens, and in 2023 the highest tax rates now approach 40% for those in the top-tier. Those in the middle-class also pay an increasing amount of taxes compared to the early 1900s (Internal Revenue Service, 2023a). Importantly, too, social programs and taxes have greatly expanded the role and reach of this government and its citizens, bringing a level of scrutiny (and, in some cases, distrust) based on its functions and intentions.

Society, too, has struggled to maintain some level of authority and respect during these changing times. Religions were once viewed with near-universal regard, but that is falling. Social clubs were flooded with members, but most struggle to maintain their relevance. Neighborhoods associations once populated cities, and now they are nearly extinct. Same with charities – ones today have fewer volunteers to promote their laudable endeavors. Then there is the media.

The media, too, has exasperated these societal challenges. In far too many occasions, the media seems to glorify the bad and neglect the good, believing the bad drives viewership and advertising dollars. It does in the short term yet affects the media's credibility in the long term. Moreover, the media (print, television, and social media) seem to delight in stories about conflict and dissension between religions, genders, the rich and powerful, and Democrats and Republications. Anything that portrays tension, even hate, and showcases differences rather than commonalities seems to lead the words they say and write. No wonder compromise seems non-existent.

We are a republic of differences, not only in terms of race but of religions, cultures, dreams, and traditions. For 200 years, citizens pursued their interests and had a level of respect for others that pursued their interests. They may not have agreed with those pursuits, but did not judge, interfere, or denigrate those pursuing them to the degree that is done so today. Some who vote Republican can no longer talk to those that vote Democrat; some of one religion cannot associate with those of another religion. Republicans now flock to Florida while Democrats stay in California, and some flee to the suburbs while others remain in the cities. Sad.

The ability to compromise – to understand one's choice and appreciate their right to have one – is rapidly fading into obscurity. Instead, encouraged by politicians and the media, single-interest groups and well-funded individuals, there is a "winner take all" and "take no prisoners" approach to promoting what one person, and one group, believes is the right thing to say and the right thing to do. Those who believe otherwise are degraded and demonized, not understood and appreciated for their different and diverse opinions. It is a deliberate strategy by some to divide this country and its people, an effort that has sadly proven wildly effective yet terribly destructive.

It doesn't have to be this way…

...we do not have government by the majority.
we have government by the majority who participate."

Former President Thomas Jefferson

CHAPTER 3

CONTRIBUTE

Leaving high school at 16 because his grades were too low and school policy mandated students maintain an acceptable Grade Point Average (GPA), he took one of the jobs available to young men of his age without a diploma: a garbageman. Back in those days, a garbageman was a brutal profession. Each person needed to carry the garbage of 3 to 4 houses *before* dumping it into the garbage truck, necessitating great strength. That young man worked for more than 30 years as a garbageman, over time buying enough shares in the company to become a major stockholder. He participated as an employee, and contributed as an owner. That high-school dropout became my father.

When she was 3 and her sister was 5, her father left her mother for a far younger woman. Though he had a solid career at Lockheed and was rewarded handsomely while employed there, that man never paid a penny of child support. He never sent his daughters any money, forcing his former wife and her children to subsist in abject poverty, subsiding only on welfare and the good nature of family and friends. He also never sent any birthday cards, or notes of any kind, during this childhood. He was quite a terrible man.

Remember that this was during the 1940s when there were few opportunities for women to make a living, and single mothers of that age were treated horrifically by others. But that 3-year-old girl worked hard as she grew, securing 2 and 3 jobs when she was able to, balancing her school demands with the expectation that she would participate toward the family's finances. After her marriage at a young age, she worked full-time during the day for a school district and then as a telephone operator for an answering service during the evening. She did all this while raising 4 children and helping her husband with their other businesses. That 3-year-old girl became my mother.

And what became of her sister, the 5-year-old who distinctly remembers her father leaving and never returning for almost 20 years? That girl also worked while she was going to school, which was not a common occurrence in those days. She married young and quickly had two children, as was the expectation in those days. But what was not customary was for this young lady to open a home bookkeeping and accounting business to bring money into her family, eventually using that money (with her husband) to buy farms, bowling alleys, and resorts. That young 5-year-old was, and is, my aunt.

I once wrote that "everyone has something, and what we do with that something, can make us a somebody." My father and mother certainly had challenging young lives, but they worked hard, saved money, took a risk on a business, and over many years, eventually made it. Their story is not that different than many who came to this country from somewhere else, in another time. My father's family came from Italy, and my mother's family came from Ireland, both without financial resources of any scope. They did not have anything, but they had something – a drive, a motivation, a hunger for something different for themselves and their eventual family. They came from nothing and wished for something which, in so many ways, typifies the American spirit.

That hope, that promise, is what makes this place so unique and its inhabitants (from every age and corner of the world) so fortunate. It is a system that affords a person the opportunity to make it, if they so CHOOSE to make it; if they take the chances that are before them. No matter the lands where we are born, or our race or gender or orientation, this country has, and continues to offer, an opportunity that so few other places offered at the time, or maybe since. One such person who took advantage of his opportunities, who came from nothing to be something, was a man by the name of Frederick Douglass.

• •

Frederick Douglass

Quick question: who was the first African American to receive a vote for president of the United States? That happened 150 years ago, at the Republican convention, and that man was Frederick Douglass. But it was not the only accomplishment from a man who came to define a generation and inspire those in another; a man who did more to realize his ideals than nearly any other.

Born into slavery, he fought for freedom for himself and others, becoming one of the first to do so. He was aided by many in this pursuit, including the wife of the person he worked for. She taught him the alphabet, against her husbands' wishes, and that instilled in him a love and appreciation of education. He then used his spectacular oratory gifts and renowned written skills, to highlight the fallacies and morality of subjugating an entire people to the will of others. He spoke truth to power, before that phrase was ever uttered to the powerful by the powerless.

How successful was Mr. Douglass during a time when African Americans were deliberately and consciously excluded from the paths toward opportunity? Consider the following: he opened an African American school in Baltimore, MD, served as the president of a bank, and even met President Lincoln in an effort to secure fair pay for black soldiers (Basker, 2018). Almost unbelievable!

Though Mr. Douglass believed in fairness and equality, he believed both were achieved through work. He once said, "we may explain success mainly by one word, and that word is work! work!! work!!! work!!!! (Frederick Douglass Heritage, 2023). He believed inequities were wrong, and then worked to ensure they were overcome and outlawed. Over a century later, the words and work of Mr. Douglass continue to inspire others to do the same.

"people might not get all they work for in this world,
but they must certainly work for all they get."
Frederick Douglass

• •

This is a country built by the contributions of its people, from those here before the republic was founded, to those who immigrated from foreign lands, along with those born to both of those groups. What brought those people here? Quite simply: hope and promise. The hope that we can become anything we want, from the local butcher to the president of the United States of America. In fact, most presidents came from humble, even poor, backgrounds including Ronald Reagan, Richard Nixon, and Harry S. Truman. Quite a list.

They also came because of the promise that if we work for it, we have a chance to make it. Many have done so, because this is one of the few places where there is a chance. That is what this country offered its citizens, but what should the citizens offer their country? John F. Kennedy famously said during his inaugural speech as president of the United States that we should "ask not what your country can do for you. Ask what you can do for your country." He meant that we all have a responsibility to further the interests of our people and our country, if we are to continue to offer the same hope and promise to those that follow our paths toward these lands. In particular, a country – any country – should expect, require, and demand its citizens meet the following obligations, and perform the following duties, as the price of admission. These include the duty to work, the duty to participate, the duty to learn, and the duty to contribute. Each is discussed in detail here:

Duty to work. As mentioned earlier, my dad was a garbageman. My mom spent many decades working in a school district, then for the federal government, as a secretary (a term rarely used today, the more common title is administrative assistant). Though they were major shareholders of the garbage company, they also started a farming and ranching business, ventured into apartment complexes and commercial buildings, and eventually purchased fast-food restaurants. How did they do this? They worked hard, saved their money, and took a chance. They had some help, too, and a little luck. But they made it. That is so American!

By the way, not all were successful. The apartment buildings lost money, and in some years the farm crops were destroyed by Mother Nature. But they kept going, never dissuaded or deterred, because they believed in the operative word, "next." If it didn't work out this time, it would the next time. And they never forgot that it all started with their jobs as a garbageman and a secretary. Good jobs. Decent jobs.

Countries work because their people work. The primary duty of a people, it is said, is to find gainful, productive work that in some way and in some place allows a country to meet its commitments to its people and in the community of nations. Without the teacher or poet, doctor or housekeeper, engineer or garbageman, a humanitarian would be less humane, and a civilized people would be less civilized. Work is fundamental to a functioning citizenry: some to grow the food and others to make the food; some to sweep the streets and others to patrol the streets; some to design the buildings and others to construct the building. And each person, absent any physical or mental reservations, has a duty and obligation to work.

As with other countries of the 1700 and 1800s, the United States was a place where its citizens worked. During these times, they had

57

to. Nearly all worked on farms supporting the family and the small communities in which they stayed. If a person did not work, they did not eat as there were few opportunities for public assistance other than what was provided on their own or through their family. There were churches that helped, and maybe close friends or neighbors, but it was a solitary existence almost wholly dependent on a person and their family.

As technology evolved and fewer hands were needed on the family farms, people moved to the cities to find work, to make a living. The rising manufacturing and technology sectors offered an opportunity – an opportunity to work in the rudimentary technology of that age, from sewing machines to steam locomotives, telegraphs, and telephones. Many took it, and that was the beginning of organizations, management, and employees, along with vendors, stores, and customers.

Americans have also continued to work. The percentage of the working-age population (defined as the total number of individuals aged 15 to 64 who can work) has remained remarkably steady over the past centuries. Since these statistics were first calculated in 1900, approximately 55% of the working age population held a job (United States Department of Commerce, 1944). That number may seem low, but remember that there are young adults still attending school, and those not yet 64 may have retired from the workforce at an earlier age. That was in 1900, and almost a century later the working age percentage had risen to 67%, the highest on record, mainly because women have entered the workforce in large numbers and there was a much younger population (Forbes, 2023). By 2023, the percentage of the working-age population who held a job had fallen back to 60%, still higher than in 1900 though (Trading Economics, 2023b).

Within the working age population of 2023, there are over 160 million individuals working out of a total of 207 million individuals eligible for work (Zane, 2023). That is a considerable achievement given that in 2023 there is a higher percentage of the working-age population in school than in 1900. In fact, in 1910 only 72% of children attended school, and 50% of those were still in one-room schools. It was not until 1918 that the United States required students to at least complete elementary school (Urban & Wagoner, 2004), which began the dawn of universal education. College enrollment has grown steadily over these years, too, impacting the numbers of those in the workforce. As an example, in 1965 only about 6% of the population were in colleges or universities; by 2023 that percentage had more than tripled to about 20% of the population (Statista, 2023).

As we have seen, the increase of the working age percentage working in 2023 versus 1900 is considerable given the astounding increase of those attending school, both in high school and colleges and universities. The United States remains a working country, though there are some changes in the composition of the work itself. For instance, the percentage of those working part-time has risen from 13.5% in 1968 (the first year these statistics were first collected) to approximately 17% in 2023, a modest increase in percentage, but considerable in total numbers (Nash, 2023). And currently, there are more people working as independent workers than in any recorded time: about 65 million workers now work at least part-time as independent workers, either as "gig" workers or freelancers or contractors (Small Business Labs, 2022).

The types of jobs have changed, but people are still working in them. Along with education, hard work is about the only place where a person can advance their position or status. One person who did just that was Ray Kroc:

• •

Ray Kroc

Millions had their first job at one of his restaurants. Even today more than 200,000 work at the company he founded, with another 2 million employed at one of the more than 40,000 restaurants scattered throughout the lands. Almost 70 million people visit one of his restaurants every day in almost 120 countries (McCain, 2023). You surely guessed it: that restaurant is McDonalds, and the man who founded that empire was Ray Kroc.

A high school dropout, he drove an ambulance during World War I (lying about his age so he could join). After the war he "played piano by night and sold paper cups by day" and it was through selling cups that he became intrigued by the milkshake machine (Rakitov, n.d.). He soon sold those milkshake machines, and during one sales call he met the McDonald brothers, who owned a popular hamburger restaurant. He thought it had a fantastic business model, one focusing on a simple menu and extraordinary customer service. Sensing an opportunity, in 1955 he convinced the brothers to let him franchise their restaurant.

By 1961, Ray had purchased the entire business, including its more than 100 restaurants at that time. He focused on familiar food and good prices along with standardization across restaurants. Not surprisingly, when he wrote his autobiography he titled it, *Grinding it out: The Making of McDonald's.* It was a recognition that he made it through hard work and determination. Was he lucky too? Certainly, luck was a factor, but success rarely comes from luck alone: rather, luck often comes from hard work and determination.

"luck is a dividend of sweat:
the more you sweat, the luckier you get"
Ray Kroc

· ·

Ray Kroc was a person who, like so many throughout history, was raised with a duty to work. Many, too, also felt a duty to participate, which is as important.

- **Duty to participate.** The duty to participate was not necessarily one of the founding principles of the United States. In fact, it really was not one of the founding principles of many countries during this time. Most people lived a more isolated existence, working with their family rather than in an organization. There were also few social clubs to join or schoolhouses to attend, creating a community of families rather than a community of citizens.

The advent of technology in the 1800s changed all that. Technology prompted the need for more learning and training, which necessitated people becoming more community minded and orientated. Children needed to learn to read and write, and then acquire other skills to later assume positions in factories and manufacturing plants. Cities were built, and communication channels were developed, through the movement to move beyond the farmhouse or small town was not welcome by all, and those reasons can be traced to the late 1700s.

Many are amazed to recall, or learn, that it took almost 10 months for the states to ratify the Constitution. That event did not formally occur until the state of Rhode Island voted to approve the Constitution on May 29, 1790. Before that date, many states and their people wanted to retain their independence from a national government, believing the more powerful states and certain vested interests would dominate the others (National Archives, n.d.). They did not necessarily want to participate in the wider, and broader, country that was to become the United States of America. They enjoyed their isolated existence in a small town.

Alexander Hamilton, James Madison, and John Jay worked tirelessly to change the tide of public opinion that was against the creation of a United States of America. They wrote a series of essays, 85 in total, extolling the virtues of the country. Those essays later became the *Federalist Papers,* a book that detailed how the new country would operate and function (National Constitution Center, 2023). It highlighted both the powers the country would and would not have.

It was not until those involved in creating this country acknowledged that a Bill of Rights would be created that those in the smaller states voted to approve the Constitution. The people wanted the rights granted in that bill, and these rights were central to becoming a part of the nation.

With that acknowledgment, and later vote for the Constitution, the citizens of a state became participants in a country.

That vote, in fact the principle of voting, is seen as one of the central responsibilities of a citizen. It is through this action that a person participates in the leadership and management of its territory. Without elections, a republic may eventually be led by unethical and unscrupulous people, the powerful and the special interests. But through the power of the vote, modifications were made and demands were agreed to, occurrences that may never have occurred without the requirement of a vote. The vote is the ultimate "weapon" held by the governed against those who govern them, and without that weapon, tyranny and subjugation are possible.

That said, though, the United States, as with other countries through time, has had a complicated history with voting. Originally left to the states, voting was often limited to white males who owned land, or those that passed some sort of religious test. It is inconceivable that those who created this republic – who believed that "all men are created equal...with unalienable Rights...among these are Life, Liberty and the pursuit of Happiness," did not believe that "all men" included all humans. It was not until 1870 that non-whites were allowed to vote through the passage of the 15th Amendment, almost a century after the Constitution was adopted. It took almost another 50 years for the 19th Amendment to be passed, which then finally allowed women the right to vote (McBride, 2021).

Other barriers took decades longer to address. The Voting Rights Act of 1965 eliminated poll taxes and literacy tests, and in later years legislation was passed to assist those with disabilities to vote and allow citizens to register to vote through their state motor vehicle departments (McBride, 2021). Even as these barriers have been removed, though, the percentage of eligible voters who actually vote has decreased since the 1840s. In much of the 19th century, about 80% of the population eligible to vote actually voted. We have not reached that figure in the 20th century. In 2020, about 66% of eligible votes actually voted in the presidential elections, a high figure and one that reversed a trend of largely declining vote patterns since the 1960s (McDonald, n.d.).

There remain some challenges to voting in 2023, but few of those are political ones. Issues such as childcare, work schedules, and transportation options affect some voters, but absentee ballots have mitigated part of those challenges. Political aspects can also be limiting such as the location of polling places and polling hours. Those, too, have been minimized by absentee ballots. But no matter the real or imagined challenges, it remains the responsibility of citizens to vote, and exercise their constitutional right to vote, to hold those elected and appointed to serve their interests both accountable and responsible. It is how we, as ordinary citizens, are able to exert some control over the direction of our country and, by extension, our lives.

That is why, again, it remains the obligation of people to vote. There are other obligations, too, required of each person who calls a certain plot of land their home, their country. There is an obligation to follow the laws. While we may not agree or support some of the laws in this republic – and some laws of the past have indisputably been problematic, even an abomination – laws are among the only mechanisms that a people can promote in order to create and maintain civility amongst its people. And, importantly, they must follow these laws willingly.

Thomas Jefferson understood the importance of following the law, and then not following the law. He once said that "if a law is unjust, a man is not only right to disobey it, he is obligated to do so" (Monticello, n.d.). Other than those singular issues where the law is corrupt and must be changed, it is the obligation of each citizen to faithfully follow the law, because otherwise this or any other republic would cease to exist as a democracy and infringe upon the liberty of each person. Fellow president John Adams believed that "our Constitution was made only for a moral and religious people. It is wholly inadequate to the government of any other" (National Center for Constitutional Studies, n.d.). President Adams believed that only moral people could sustain a democracy, possibly because the ability to vote benefits and advantages to certain people must be balanced against what is right and fair. To be sure, laws must be made and followed, by the people who collectively inhabit those areas covered by the law. It seems inconceivable for a state and its people to be able to thrive or survive, under any other manner.

And this includes the paying of taxes, too, which is another mechanism by which people participate. It remains the obligation of each person to pay their taxes. More importantly, every citizen must pay income tax to be a resident of this land if they are physically and mentally able to do so. They must pay something to support the basic operations of the state. Taxes are the monies we collectively, as a people, rely upon to build the roads we travel upon, police the streets we walk, and teach in the schools our children attend. Sadly, many do not contribute to income taxes.

In 2022, only about 60% of U.S. households paid income tax, meaning that fully 40% of U.S. households paid no income taxes, mainly because their income was below the threshold required to pay income taxes (Statista, 2023b). For these and other basic services that we enjoy and use, all should pay at least something toward their support, no matter how minimal. That is fair.

Besides those who do not pay any tax, there are those that do not pay their full tax – the so-called tax dodgers or tax cheats. According to Charles Rettig, the former commissioner of the Internal Revenue Service (IRS), approximately $1 trillion is lost each year by those not paying their full share of taxes (Rappeport, 2021). Given that the IRS collects about $5 trillion in income taxes a year, that means an additional 17% is lost per year, every year, due to unpaid taxes (Internal Revenue Service, 2023b). That is unfair.

There is one other aspect of income taxes that is seen as unfair, but not necessarily by all. The United States has a progressive income tax system, which means the more money one makes the higher percentage of tax they pay on that money. This results in certain individuals paying a higher *percentage* of their income on taxes than others. In 2022, for instance, the top 1% of Americans paid almost 43% of all federal income taxes, and only received 22% of the nation's gross income (Lord, 2023). The top 10% paid about 74% of all federal income taxes while collecting about 50% of the nation's income (Desilver, 2023; York, 2023). It is fair to say, given these statistics, that those with higher incomes do pay their fair share, if not more.

- **Duty to learn.** The duty to participate was not necessarily one of the founding principles of the United States. In fact, it really was not one of the founding principles of many countries during this time. Most occupied a more isolated existence, working at home rather than within an organization and with limited clubs to join. The opportunities to interact with others were infrequent, leading to a somewhat lonely day. Schooling was not a fundamental responsibility of Americans during this time, but it became their duty as the expectations to become a productive and additive member of society arose over these many years.

Interestingly, the founders had a keen understanding of the importance of education in the new republic. In 1816, Thomas Jefferson acknowledged this fact in this statement to Charles Yancey:

"every government has propensities to command
at will the liberty and property of their constituents...
but where the press is free, and every
man able to read, all is safe."
(Library of Congress, n.d.)

And so, the initial efforts to create an educational system began. The intentions, not surprisingly, were somewhat different than centuries later. The focus was to create an educated citizenry who, again according to Jefferson, could sustain democracy and provide for their own present and future. He believed that "self-government is not possible unless the citizens are educated sufficiently to enable them to exercise oversight," a statement that has only grown in importance in the present day (University of Virginia, 1817). These beliefs led to Jefferson's creation of the University of Virginia (and the United States Military Academy West Point) along with the proposal to require 3 years of schooling for both male and female children. Sadly, the latter was never passed by Congress.

By 1840, though, about 55% of children attended a primary school, and schools became more common around the early 1900s. The need to educate the citizenry to participate in the rapidly growth economy, along with the requirement to learn management and other work-related skills, prompted cultural and societal leaders like John Dewey and W.E.B. DuBois to lead these efforts. DuBois, in particular, worked to ensure schools taught more than the subjects of math and English, and that schools of higher learning focused on broader knowledges and skills, stating these schools should teach "intelligence, broad sympathy, knowledge of the world that was and is, and of the relation of men to it" (DuBois, 1903).

From those humble beginnings, education became a controlling force in American society. As in 2021, there were 55 million children attending prekindergarten through 12th grade, and another 20 million attending colleges and universities (NCES, 2022). Federal, state, and local governments spend over $15,000 for each student in kindergarten through 12th grade, totaling almost $800 billion annually (Hanson, 2022), and the nation spends almost six cents of every tax dollar received on some type of education (Trading Economics, 2023c). It may have taken a century for the United States to realize the importance of education – as with other countries – however, there is no doubt it now assumes a more prominent role in society.

So, what has the role of education become today? Two thoughts come to mind. First, we enter schools to gain the knowledge and skills necessary to labor in an often changing and undeniably dynamic place. Not only the rudimentary skills – from communicating with others to managing one's finances – but also the more advanced knowledge and skills such as finding a job and making a living. Experiences are worthwhile, but without the foundational knowledge and skills that one learns through a competent and comprehensive educational system, it is challenging if not impossible, to acquire the background to do so.

Secondly, as mentioned by Jefferson and many other wise men and women of another age, education should focus on creating a good student and person, within a good society. Through the best of education, students have the opportunity to become a more moral, spiritual, and philosophical person; one who can then use this knowledge to make a more reasoned and rational decision, one that is not selfish or self-interested, but rather more balanced and fairer, more attuned to the influences of goodness, decency, and honor.

Citizens have a duty to learn for many of these reasons. Education is meant to showcase the possibilities that exist in the world of today and the opportunities that can be created in the world of tomorrow. Through this experience we have the chance to transform our place into something unique, something greater. That is not only our intention but our expectations through education, and why governments over the lands continue to devote countless monies to these efforts.

One person who learned the lessons of possibilities and opportunities through education, and made something better through her efforts, was an inspirational woman named Helen Keller. Here is her story:

. . . .

Helen Keller

An unknown illness caused a 19-month-old Helen Keller to lose her sight and hearing, leading to an unruly childhood that lasted until she met her lifelong friend Anne Sullivan. Anne became a towering influence in Helen's life, teaching her to read and write by drawing letters in her hand for each object she touched, from water to dolls. Shortly thereafter, Helen began her mastery of the alphabet and soon moved to learning to speak (American Foundation for the Blind, n.d.).

That relationship was also the impetus for Helen to continue her education, later becoming the first deaf and blind person to graduate from college. That college was Harvard, a remarkable achievement, but she is remembered more for what she did with her education.

Helen cofounded the American Civil Liberties Union, and through the books she wrote and the speeches she gave, traveled the planet to highlight the challenges, and opportunities of those who were deaf or blind. So influential was Helen that the book about her times, *The Miracle Worker,* won the Pulitzer Prize (Britannica, 2023). Later, the movie adaptation of that book won the Academy Award for Patty Duke, the woman who portrayed Helen Keller in that film.

Helen became a true American hero, a person who enlightened others by recognizing the value of everyone, including those with disabilities.

"the two most interesting characters of the 19th century
are Napoleon and Helen Keller."
Mark Twain

• •

Helen once wrote in *The Home Magazine* that "education should train a child to use their brains, to make for themselves a place in the world" (Keller, 1934). She recognized the duty of each person to learn, to become educated. She also knew she must do something with what she had, using the unique skills and abilities, education and experiences, that she developed.

Helen Keller also knew she had a duty to contribute.

• **Duty to contribute.** What is the difference between participating and contributing? Participants vote; contributors' campaign. Participants work; contributors manage. Participants sit in the stands; contributors play on the field. Indisputably, a functioning and productive community, a fun and interesting place, needs both. Without votes no candidate is elected; without employees no managers are needed; without fans no superstars are idolized.

There are those who prefer to be the spectator, the bystander, along the roads they travel; there are others who prefer to be the candidate, the contender, within the arenas they enter. Each, at one time and in one place, is invaluable and indispensable. In reality and practice, the difference between the player and the participant is exceedingly small and often merely a question of time or place. That is because each person is given something, anything, that is different than someone else, and that difference is what makes a person a spectator in one sport and a player in another.

The greatest of Hollywood actors, those who have unbelievable wealth and astounding fame, can be seen browsing a museum and wondering at the artistry of a painter. I am constantly amazed to see the greats watching the other greats do what they are best at. We see tennis greats Rafael Nadal and Roger Federer sitting in stadiums transfixed at the skills of football superstars. Or former presidents Bill Clinton and Donald Trump clamoring to play with legendary golfers Tiger Woods and Phil Mickelson. Why? No matter their own accomplishments, these famous athletes and politicians respect and revere what others have to offer, knowing that every person has something to offer, and that is what makes us unique and special, interesting and exciting. This fact changes the very disposition of a person from one of jealousy and envy, to one of appreciation and admiration.

There are also the most unskilled of laborers, the ones with the lowest pay and perceived status, who can be seen leading the fundraising efforts for the new community center. Then there is the chief executive officer of a multi-national conglomerate, a person of immense power and privilege, who can be seen playing the flute at a local tavern on a Monday night. Each person has a role to play, each person is important in their own place, and each person can not only participate in their specific area but then contribute in another as well.

Thankfully we are not segmented in perpetuity as either the watcher or the watched. It is a matter of time and place, ability and desire. The best of individuals, and the best of communities, are those where each citizen has a unique gift to share; something that no other person has and can attain regardless of the training or effort expended. The hope, for those we live among, is that we all use those traits and characteristics, talents and capabilities, that make us unique and interesting, fascinating and intriguing, so that at some point and in some place we become the contributor rather than the participant. That may not happen today, or tomorrow, but maybe someday soon. Too many wait too long to contribute, and that is a shame.

No matter the job or age, if someone has the physical and mental ability to contribute, they should; they must. The expectation, if not the requirement, is that those from the past provide the advice and counsel for those who come next. That no matter your age or accomplishments of the past, you continue to contribute to the betterment of your state; of your community. Sadly, there are some who believe that after years of work it is time to "stop and smell the roses," to enjoy their remaining years. Again, that is a shame. It is precisely at that age, with their years of education and experience, that a person may have the most value to a community.

While some are climbing the ladder to achieve some goal, other individuals have done just that, and that knowledge of "how to" and "where to" and "when to" can be instructive and constructive to the success of those who follow. There are those who attain a position of importance – from a police chief to a maintenance laborer, a design engineer to a parole officer – and then retire to pursue more recreational adventures, which is their right, no doubt. But so much of their history, from how they made it to how they kept it, would be of incontestable value to those who follow, to those who assume those positions previously held by them and others. This is not the only way an individual can contribute, no matter the number of years they have remaining, but certainly most important to consider.

It is a lesson well-learned by the late actress Bette Davis, who once stated that "the key to life is accepting challenges. Once someone stops doing this, he's dead" (Hall, 2022). And she had more to say:

• •

Bette Davis

Without question, Bette Davis was one of the great actors in cinematic history. At one point she had more Academy

Award nominations for Best Actor than any person in Hollywood. She also won two Academy Awards for Best Actress, among the very few who have won two Best Actor Oscars. Her 10 nominations still stand as the third most in history, a remarkable feat more than 30 years after her death in 1989.

Her talent, along with her dedication and drive, has long been admired by nearly every actor or actress who has followed. But it was not an easy path for Bette Davis. Her father once told her to remember how "unimportant you are," a sobering statement that could have paralyzed another young person yet served to motivate Bette to "conquer the world," as she later wrote in one of her two autobiographies (Meares, 2020). She obviously did not have a close relationship with her father.

But she prevailed, and then conquered. Almost until her dying breath, Bette Davis learned, worked, and contributed. She studied the craft of moviemaking and, along the way, battled with powerful studio heads such as the founder of Warner Brothers Studios, Jack Warner. She wanted richer parts but he refused to give them to her, so she left for England. He sued and she lost, and she later stated that "I am a woman. I was told I had no right to fight like a man" (Movies Staff, 2022). But she stood her ground and became the Bette Davis of legend.

She learned, and worked, and contributed right up until the end. She had something to say, and something to do, and we are grateful that she shared both with us all.

"she did it the hard way."
self-chosen epitaph on the grave of Bette Davis

• •

Bette Davis lived a remarkable life, and she did it the hard way.

And there were many others who felt a sense of duty, and it became their honor, to contribute something to their current and subsequent generations. Not all were famous like Mahatma Gandhi, who led his country from British rule in the 1940s and inspired countless others such as Martin Luther King, Jr. to follow in his non-violent example. Martin Luther King, Jr. once said that the Gandhian philosophy was, "the only morally and practically sound method open to oppressed people in their struggle for freedom" (Stanford University, n.d.). Then there was Ludwig van Beethoven, possibly the greatest music composer in history, who produced over 700 works of music during his time, defining the art of musical composition that still exists today, all while losing his hearing during his most productive periods (Cabrera, 2021). Finally, we remember Johann Gutenberg, the founder of the printing press in the mid-1400, whose invention of movable type allowed the written word to be disseminated everywhere, sending research and knowledge to inventors, chemists, and engineers to build upon the thoughts of others. This one invention allowed millions of citizens to learn to read, raising the possibility that the most ordinary of people could become the most extraordinary of contributors (Lemelson-MIT, (n.d.).

Summary

Societies were created, sustained, and then recreated not because its citizens believed in individuality, but rather, commonality. This need for commonality is a virtual requirement of a people and is manifested in the expectation those living within its borders 'do something' besides have a sense of community, that they contribute to the advancement of their people and their country, if not the planet. It is this expectation to "do something' that is displayed in their duty to work, duty to participate, and duty to learn.

When the United States was founded, like other countries, a small group of energetic individuals banded together to create something safer and freer; one that offered more promise in the coming years than the debilitating misery offered in the past years. That was the belief and hope, which once realized, necessitated a continued sense of sacrifice and adventure by an inspired yet unknowing populace. The duty to work may be paramount in this effort, but the people have other responsibilities, including to participate in the governance and support of the republic through voting, following the laws, and paying their taxes. Sharing their unique talents toward the benefit of others is another duty, as is the duty to learn, to acquire the knowledge and skills necessary to further their own pursuits, along of those that follow. And finally, they have a duty to contribute one's own talents to create something different, and maybe something better.

That is what makes a country a home.

learn what we can,
share what we know,
and contribute to something good.

CHAPTER 4

GRACIOUS

When some think of gracious, or grace, we often think of the way people move or act or talk. Something physical. We watch the grace of a ballet dancer as they move across the stage. They glide as much as move, in an effortless manner that reflects the elegance of the performance, and the style of the person. We wonder at the demeanor of a person who acts with composure and dignity. They captivate our attention through their bearing and conduct, traits of a person with perfect deportment. And then we hear the grace in the voice of someone who talks in a bright and cheerful tone. The soothing and comforting intonations of such confident people command our attention and respect.

Unquestionably, when we think of grace we often reflect on certain individuals of prominence. Grace Kelly comes to mind, the near-mythical former Academy Award-winning actress who became a princess of Monaco, dying at a young age in a tragic automobile accident. She was more than an actress and a princess, though. Her myth was enhanced by the legion of causes that she supported, including her lifelong dedication to the Red Cross, which raised millions for the cause and promoted its good works far beyond the borders of the principality of Monaco. Maybe her name "Grace" had something to do with her image, which evokes a serene woman of immeasurable warmth.

Former first lady Jacqueline Kennedy Onassis has also been seen as a person of great grace, always perfectly dressed and poised, presenting herself as a woman of class and distinction. Her father always told her to "hold something back" because people would be more interested in what that was. She did, and they were. Former British deputy prime minister Willie Whitelaw, too, had a graceful presence. A man of immense charm, his grace was even more pronounced given that he attained the heights of British politics in doing so.

He was, at one time or another, the Deputy Prime Minister, and the Leader of the House of Lords. Upon his death *The Guardian* wrote he was a "genial man, famously serene in the heat of political battle." They also said it was a "foolish politician who underestimated his skills," underlying the belief that nice guys finish last. Even his former foes spoke well of him, as former British prime minister Tony Blair remarked upon Willie's death "he was a genuinely decent man" (Reed, 1999). High praise from an opponent in the political arena.

Of course, the Holy Bible speaks often of grace, too. James 4:6 says that "God opposes the proud but gives grace to the humble," and 1 Corinthians 15:10 states that "by the Grace of God I am what I am" (Crossway, 2022). More famously, that last phrase has been reworded by many to read, "there but for the grace of God." It was the English reformer John Bradford who in 1553 first stated those words as he saw a prisoner being led to their execution. He was expressing his appreciation that his fate was not the same as that prisoner, acknowledging that without some twist of circumstance or divine intervention his destiny could have been similar to that of the prisoner (Coombs, 2023). Many more have uttered those same words, noting their circumstances could have been so different if not for some luck, or good fortune, that they encountered for some unknown reason.

Grace is not limited to those of prominence, those who have won an Academy Award, served as the First Lady of the United States, or as the Deputy Prime Minister of Great Britain. It is a uniquely common trait, one that can be learned by any person, of any age, of any social status, and in any corner of this Earth. And the traits that can best represent a person of grace include the "3 C's and an F," with the C's representing courtesy, civility, and cheer, and the F representing friendliness. Each of these traits is discussed in detail throughout the remaining parts of this chapter.

- **Courtesy**. Courtesy is known by several other names, including basic manners and common decencies. Notice the terms "basic" and "common." These allude to the fact that there are aspects that should be associated with each person, that they form the basis of what we expect from those we meet, and of what others should expect when they meet us. Regrettably for some, these courtesies are less basic and common than they have been in the past, even surpassed in some areas by the words rude, cruel, and selfish. It never has to be that way.

To start, a courteous person is one who has manners. Manners are often taught by parents as we are raised, and they generally follow us throughout our years. Manners are, in many ways, basic to our way of life. They are often the way in which we talk, move or act, and they are often customary to the place in which we call home. For instance, in the United States some of the manners that are basic include:

- o during meals, removing elbows from the table and chewing with one's mouth closed;
- o when meeting others, stating it is "a pleasure to meet you" or "so nice to make your acquaintance";
- o In conversation with others, using the phrases "please" and "thank you" and "excuse me";
- o a well-mannered person does not use foul language, nor do they speak ill or dismissive of others;
- o finally, not interrupting others in conversation or speaking too loudly or forcefully.

These manners may be basic to some, but they are symbolic of a cultured, even polished, person and society.

Another trait of a courteous person is deference. What is a deferential person? It is a person who holds the door for others, walks last into a room, stands up when elders walk in the room, and refers to their elders as sir and ma'am. Contrary to what others may define, interpret, or perceive, a deferential person does not denote one who is "less than" someone else but rather one who is "more than" someone else. Deference is a great show of respect toward someone else not only of their opinion but of their personage. Even to those we disagree with or may be in conflict with, a show of deference indicates we recognize and appreciate their status and stature, and this may not be the issue or time to continue one's opposition.

In some, if not many, ways deference treating others better than they treat you, in a more hospitable manner. It is a sign of a confident and sophisticated person, a positive and admirable trait among the most enlightened of people.

- **Civility.** There is an interesting story about George Washington who, when he was 14 years old, read a book called, *Rules of Civility and Decent Behavior in Company and Conversation.* That book, translated from the French, presented the actions and behavior that a person should display during their course of personal interactions with others, including in business (Nadler & Schulman, 2006). Some of these rules included "show not yourself glad at the misfortune of another though he were you enemy" and "when a man does all he can, though it succeeds not well, blame not him that did it" (Providence Forum, n.d.). Mr. Washington remembered, and followed, these rules when he entered into the political fray, including during his time as the first president of the United States, and it served him and his country well.

Originally, the term civility comes from the Latin word *civilis*, meaning "relating to public life, befitting a citizen" with the Cambridge Dictionary adding that civility is "respectful behavior between people" (Cambridge Dictionary, n.d.; Vocabulary.com, n.d.). It seems rational, then, for George Washington to read *Rules of Civility and Decent Behavior in Company and Conversation* and then apply it to his governmental service and leadership. Civility refers to how individuals should relate to others in public places, how they interact not only with their governmental representatives but with those they encounter through their everyday interactions and conversations. And the operative word here, in these occasions, is polite.

Being civil is simple when there is little at stake. It is only when the stakes are high, and the consequences unsure or dire, that the notion of civility is greatly tested. The more unfavorable the past, the more complicated the relationship, and the more divisive the issue, then civility seems to fade. Losing a client to a rival makes for an uncomfortable meeting among rivals; losing a client of significance can make for a combative meeting. Losing an argument to a friend can strain a relationship; losing an argument to a foe can cause a ruptured relationship. The nature of the situation is important, but the consequences can be more problematic. The more to win or lose, the more civility will be tested.

Sports is a good analogy in relation to civility. From an early age most are taught to be a "good loser," meaning that when the battle is done, both the winner and loser should display a level of civility toward their opponent. You always, always, shake the hand of your opponent, for instance, no matter the level of your disappointment. The greatest tennis tournament, The Wimbledon Championships in London, England, displays a quote as the players enter the famed Centre Court stadium to play their match. The poem is from the great English poet Rudyard Kipling, who once wrote the following in his poem titled *If:*

> "if you can meet with Triumph and Disaster,
> and treat those two imposters just the same..."
> (Wimbledon, 2018)

That is the definitive definition of sportsmanship, and by extension civility. It is about winning and losing, with style and dignity. Some exhibit this trait more than others. The two-time Wimbledon Champion Stefan Edberg has a number of nicknames, one being affectionately known as the *Blonde Adonis,* but the one he appreciates most is *The Graceful Elegance.* He was, and is, so beloved for his level of sportsmanship that the Association of Tennis Professionals, the organization to which all male tennis players belong, renamed its sportsmanship award the Stefan Edberg Sportsman Award. After Mr. Edberg won the sportsmanship award five times, the ATP renamed the award after him. That award represents the best of sportsmanship, that whether we win or lose, we treat our opponent and the game, with equal civility. That is the standard he set not only of elegance but of civility (Gatto, 2018).

Without question, civility challenges even the most seasoned of individuals, let alone political leaders such as George Washington. Another person, in more recent times, who displayed a level of civility in the course of her duties to her nation is the recently deceased Queen Elizabeth II. She served more than 70 years on the English throne, through many tumultuous times and events, until her eventual death in 2022 at the age of 96.

• •

Queen Elizabeth II

Kings and queens are becoming relics of a bygone era. At one time nearly every country was ruled by a monarch. By 2023, though, only 40 countries were represented by a king or queen, or about 7.5% of the Earth's population (though 14 of those countries recognized the English king as their head of state). This is a dramatic fall from about 35% of the population whose head of state was a crowned monarch in the early 1950s (Zumbrum, 2022).

Monarchies are intended to represent the triumphs of their country's past, the advancements of the country's present, and the hopes for the country's future. They also represent those traits and characteristics most admired by their people. Few monarchs represented their country and their people more skillfully and artfully than Queen Elizabeth II.

She maintained a level of importance and influence throughout her years because of the manner in which she comported herself. Her motto was, "never explain, never complain," and she followed that dictum through the many challenges she faced. Even when she was required to meet foreign dictators and despots, including Romanian Nicolae Ceausescu and Zimbabwean Robert Mugabe, she did so, understanding her duties and obligations.

Quite possibly her greatest example of civility was when she met former Irish Republican Army Commander Martin McGuinness, who was involved in the murder of her husband's uncle, the Lord Mountbatten (Memmott, 2012). Yet in her capacity as monarch, she met this man and shook his hand, showing people throughout her realm that forgiveness was an essential part of humanity. That was statesmanship.

She had class, dignity, and grace. We were fortunate, too, to learn civility from her time as well.

. . . .

- **Cheer**. The last few years have undoubtedly strained the most positive and cheerful of people. The COVID pandemic altered the very nature of society, from the income we make to the places we work and to the people we meet. It was a generational event of catastrophic proportions, and its lasting impact remains years after these events have passed.

But the lack of cheer in many began far before the pandemic.

In 2022, Gallup published a book titled *Blind Sport: The Global Rise of Unhappiness and How Leaders Missed it*. It highlighted where the global rise of unhappiness had risen considerably from 2006 to 2021. Surely the pandemic had an impact, but the important aspect of that study was that unhappiness had been rising steadily for nearly 15 years before the pandemic. The authors of that book concluded that unhappiness was the result of certain individuals able to live a great life, and others not able to do so (Clifton, 2022). In other words, it is within our control to live a happy life or an unhappy life.

Again, though, why has it decreased so appreciatively just in the last 15 years despite the many advancements during those years? From developments in communications to transportation, medicines to social relations, the previous and current years offer tremendous promise to many. Few decades have seen such profound change since the first two decades of the 21st century. Nevertheless, contentment and happiness have fallen, and the reasons may be more about the people themselves than the circumstances.

There have been wars and earthquakes, depressions and tsunamis, from the last century and, most assuredly, into the next. Yet we move on. Sameness may not exist from one age to the next, but there does return a sense of continuity or normality that defines those of and during that period. Life really does go on, just a bit different than it did previously. We must adapt and adjust, and the factor most critical to whether a person can or cannot do so is attributed to their disposition and manifested in their attitude. That person is content and happy, positive and cheerful, because they follow three simple rules. These are:

o   First, they see the good in anybody and anything. Before they meet someone or enter a situation, they first look for something good, and inevitably, it is found. Whether it is the smile of the person they meet, or the sunny disposition of their character. It is one reason I follow the philosophy to "always look for the good along the road of life." From flowers to forests, adventure lands to amusement parks, there is something good to find through all we encounter if only we choose to look for it.

o   Second, do the best with what we have. The joyful are those who do the best with what they have – they leave nothing on the field other than their best effort, and only then can they walk away knowing they tried, they did all they could, and nothing else was left. While we cannot, in most cases, determine a win or loss, we can determine our effort, and that realization is what gives a person peace and satisfaction, contentment and happiness.

o   Third nothing lasts forever. Just as no one has it all, no one gets to keep it all either, at least for too long. The champion of today is often the loser of tomorrow. History is littered with those that were good and great at one time, but then have fallen or are forgotten in another. Some of the great are lifting the championship trophy one day, and standing in line at the grocery store the next. We see the sad pictures of Bjorn Borg, the greatest tennis player of his era, forced to sell his Wimbledon trophies to raise money. Or his fellow Wimbledon tennis champion Boris Becker, who went from the glory of winning to the horror of losing as he served his time in jail for tax evasion.

Nothing lasts. The happy are those who enjoy the struggle to the top, the rewards once there, and the opportunity back down to reflect about past victories and plan future battles.

A cheerful disposition is developed and retained, more by an individual's self-awareness, self-belief, self-respect, and self-worth. It is about how one interprets the good and the bad that happens in one's life – nearly everyone has experienced something similar, yet their impressions and interpretations of that event may be marketably, and more positively, viewed by one person than the other. Our journeys may not always be grand nor great, but in retrospect and reflection we all have goods and bads, achievements and failures, and hits and misses. In the end, it comes down to attitude and perspective. It is what we remember, what we focus upon, and what we dream, for that determines the happiness and cheer that we reflect upon ourselves and project upon those we meet along our travels.

- **Friendly**. There are many aspects of grace, and one of the more compelling is the notion of favor, of help, and of love. It is about extending a feeling of importance and worth to those who may not have it, but without a doubt, need it. This is where the phrase "there but for the grace of God go I" comes from – that we are hopefully more worthy than others. It does not mean that we are superior to others, only that we experience more advantageous circumstances and situations than others.

Another aspect of grace is its "charming or attractive trait or characteristic" (Holcomb, 2022). It is something that we see in ourselves, but also want to see in others. It is something we want to exhibit toward others, and something we want to receive from others as well. Along with favor, help and love, grace appears to be the definitive longing for companionship. Those who exhibit the best of grace also exhibit the best of friendship. Yet, in some ways – and actually in too many ways – we have shied away from companionship, and moved away from friendships, over these last years. Consider the following:

o   60% of U.S. consumers order delivery or takeout once a week (Bennett, 2023). It seems people do not want to eat together much anymore.

o   38% of employees did some, or all, of their work from home in 2022 (Bureau of Labor Statistics, 2022). People seem less, dramatically less, inclined to work in the same office with others anymore.

o   Membership in most fraternal associations has fallen dramatically in the last years. The Elks' membership is down from 1.6 million in 1976 to 750,000 in 2020 (nsn2020, 2020). Others have lost more: the Masons have lost 3 million members since the 1950s, the Moose Lodge is down 40% since 1986, and the Shriners lost 50% since 1990 (Cabell, 2017; Flynn, 2018). We plainly are not associating with many, or even a few, individuals outside of the workplace or outside of the home.

o   29% of people who spent several evenings with a neighbor each month in 2018, down from 44% in 1974. It gets worse: in 2017 only 54% of Americans actually talked to their neighbor a couple times a month, down from 71% in 2008

(Schweikert, 2019). Sadly, there are those who are not even aware of who their neighbors are.

- o 42% of Americans attended a church at least once a month in 2018, down from 57% in 1972 (United States Congress, (2019). Praying together seems less like an American pastime than in the past.

- o 55% of Americans donated to charity in 2014 versus 66% in 2000, and the percentage of American volunteers reached a 15-year low in 2015, falling to 25% in that year, down from 29% in 2001 (University of Maryland, 2018). A sad commentary on a once-giving nation.

- o 56 minutes a day is all the average American over the age of 15 spends in some sort of socializing or communicating. That is less than one-third the amount of time these individuals spend watching television each day, and about the same time they spend playing computer games (Bureau of Labor Statistics, 2022b). It seems people do not want to even talk with anyone on a consistent or continual basis any longer.

- o Finally, almost 60% of those who died in 2022 were cremated, a figure that is expected to read over 80% in the coming years. This compares to less than 4% who were cremated in 1960 (LaMotte, 2020; National Cremation, n.d.). Even upon death, we seem less included to spend time amongst others.

This may be the most unfortunate instance of the fall of grace; the lack of friends and friendships one has throughout their lifetime. A 2021 study by the *New York Post* found that in a land of nearly 340 million people, almost half of all Americans reported having fewer than 3 close friends; in 1990, only 27% of Americans had three or fewer close friends (Cost, 2021). Even during the COVID pandemic years, when one may assume that people would turn to their friends for comfort and joy, that figure continued to fall.

Are Americans alone in this less personal and more isolated place? Fortunately, no. There are other countries whose populace and population are more hospitable and welcoming, to their fellow citizens as well as strangers. In numerous rankings of countries deemed the most cordial, affable, and friendly throughout the lands, there are few that seem to appear on most lists. Portugal, for one, seems to appear toward the top of these lists. Though its gross domestic product per capita is one of the lowest among like countries and unemployment is high, it remains one of the safest countries to visit and live, and its people among the warmest and most inviting (Dermody, 2023; Sunde-Brown, 2021; U.S. News and World Report, 2022).

Scotland, too, ranks high in terms of friendly places to live and visit. The city of Glasgow, Scotland was named the planet's friendliest city in 2002, which may be due as much to its vast amount of green space throughout the city as to the kindness exhibited by its inhabitants (Dickinson, 2022; Oliver, 2022). Then there is the Philippines, which like Portugal is a poorer country yet its population is often regarded among the most genial. The 2022 Conde Nast review of friendliest countries lists the Philippines as the 10th most friendly city because of its hospitable nature and genuine warmth (Calieno, 2023). Quite impressive.

But there is one that seems to remain on top of many, if not most, lists, and that is the lands of New Zealand. Here may be why:

• •

New Zealand

Affectionately known as Kiwis, New Zealanders are known as among the most affable and genial people on the planet. They have a laid back "all is good" type attitude that permeates their interactions not only with their fellow countrymen but with foreigners too. It has always been an in-demand place to visit, with their inhabitants possessing a "relaxed vibe" that says we are "not rushed, and have time for you" (Owen, 2023). We are certainly welcome there.

Surely one of the most beautiful places to visit, there is something more about New Zealand that appeals to the masses. This relaxed vibe comes from its founding hundreds of years ago from the Maori people, who subscribed to the concept of manaakitanga, which is Maori for hospitality. The culture and traditions, passed from one time to the next, pursue a generosity of spirit and friendliness of heart (Conde Nast Traveller, 2022). It is unique.

The Lord of the Rings was filmed there, and extreme sports such as bungee jumping and zorbing are played there (Dermody, 2022). Stunning vistas are attractive to view, but laid-back and good-natured people are the reason New Zealand ranks amongst the best. They are THE example of a generous and kind people.

"she'll be right"
New Zealander expression meaning
'things will work out'

• •

The culture and spirit of New Zealand is reminiscent of the theme song for the legendary television show *Cheers*. The show, about a group who are "making their way through the world today" and, at the end of the day, stop in the neighborhood bar to have a drink or two. The bar is more than a watering hole to have a beer, but rather a place where all are welcome. In fact, several lines of that theme song, played at the beginning of each episode, reflect its hope:

"Sometimes you want to go

Where everybody knows your name,
and they're already glad you came.

You want to be where you can see,
our troubles are all the same
You want to be where everyone knows your name."
(Lyrics on Demand, n.d.)

Scotland, the Philippines, New Zealand, and the theme from *Cheers,* all evoke the same thought: friendship. You are treated as a friend in Scotland, the Philippines, and New Zealand, and closer to home, we are treated as a friend when we enter the *Cheers* bar. Friendship may be as foreign as it is universal; foreign in that we have fewer of them, yet universal in that wherever we go, the search for friends is never ending. And friendship begins with the generous soul of a kind person.

Kind people are those who smile even when they are alone, who offer the uncommon courtesies of "Hello, how are you doing today?" and "Take care... such a pleasure to see you" to all they meet, who extend the uncommon decencies of "Let me help you" before they are asked, who treat the king the same as they treat the pawn, and who never miss the opportunity to help someone else reach his or her dreams, even if it costs them the opportunity to reach their own. The kind person is that rare find indeed.

The good news is that anyone and everyone can become a kind person—and, at the very least, a kinder person today than he or she was yesterday. To do so, a person should focus on three specific traits beginning with holding a sunny disposition. A sunny disposition starts with what we think and how we feel, and those thoughts and feelings are manifested in what we say and how we act. Those with a sunny disposition believe in the best in others, even when they do not believe in the best in themselves.

Second, treat others better than we are treated. If the kind person is that rare find, the temptation could be to treat others as they treat us. To treat others better than they treat us—even when they are disrespectful or rude—takes an extraordinary person, one who is confident, considerate, and compassionate. They are kind, and at the other end of the spectrum are those who are unbearably sad, for "they have to live that life," a future of destructive thoughts and malicious actions. The good person never responds to negativity with negativity but rather has a genuine sadness for those who have chosen to live that type of life.

Third is having a giving heart. The kind person is one who gives more than they take and helps more than they are helped. They find true happiness in seeing others attain their ambitions, even if it costs the delay in reaching their own ambitions, or in not reaching their ambitions at all.

In truth, we meet many more genuinely nice and kind people on our path. These people think of others before themselves, of the greater good rather than the personal good, and appreciate the good fortune of others rather than bemoaning their own fate. It is often, as we have mentioned earlier, more of what we look for than of what we see. There are truly special people that we meet, and they are the personification of kindhearted people. They are the people who become our friends, and we are fortunate for that circumstance.

Summary

When some, if not most, think of a graceful person they conjure up visions of a ballerina or figure skater, those who use their bodies to create a fluid, beautiful presence in the arena. Those who exhibit grace toward others have a similar presence. Fluid, yes. Beautiful, definitely. And courteous, civil, cheerful, and friendly. These are the qualities that epitomize class and dignity.

We hope to meet and become a person of grace. To be courteous to those we like and those we don't; to be civil in discussions we enjoy and those we detest; to be cheerful in the best of circumstances and the worst; to be a friend to those who want it, and those who need it. The graceful people, and the lands they inhabit, are a welcome respite from an, at times, quarrelsome and hostile place, and their presence is one characteristic that helps make a good place, a great place.

if I'm a duck,
and someone calls me a donkey,
it doesn't make me a donkey.

CHAPTER 5

GRATEFUL

Andrew Carnegie was a soaring figure in history. At one point he was among the wealthiest of Americans, with a net worth so vast he rivaled anyone in history. But toward the end of his years he wrote a book called *The Gospel of Wealth* that made the formative statement, "the man who dies thus rich dies disgraced (Carnegie Corporation of New York, n.d.) By that time, he started to give away his massive fortune to, among others, the founding of Carnegie-Mellon University and the construction of more than 2,500 libraries across the planet. Oh, and he built Carnegie Hall, a performance hall still enjoyed by thousands in New York City, and donated thousands of organs to various churches.

He fulfilled his mission to give away most of what he spent his years trying to accumulate. Upon his death, his wife kept their personal assets, and his daughter was given a small trust. But that trust was not sufficient to maintain her style of living and she eventually had to sell her townhouse. It was too costly to maintain (Sorvino, 2014). By that time, the fortune was gone, distributed to the far corners of Earth in the belief that his money could be used for something more than the personal interests of his small family. He was not mean and truly loved his family but believed in using his wealth for more noble and honorable ambitions, and undoubtedly he succeeded.

Mr. Carnegie was grateful to those who helped him attain the position of influence he then maintained for most of his life. His bequests showed his gratitude for what he had been given – the opportunity to do something of consequence in his time, and he wanted to afford others that same opportunity. He succeeded, as did so many others whose names still echo in the halls of conversation from Vanderbilt to Duke to Stanford to Rockefeller, and in the current generations there are the Zuckerbergs and the Paul Allen's, the Bill

Gates' and the Walton family (of the famous Walmart department stores). All were people of immense wealth who shared, at least in part, Carnegie's recognition that something must be given back by the current generation so that the next generation may find it easier to get ahead, and then to realize their responsibility to do the same for those after them.

Gratitude is not a singular American trait, and gratitude is not something that is only exhibited by those who have immense wealth. There are many people of ordinary means who left an extraordinary legacy through their words, because of their actions, and by deeds. These people serve meals for the hungry, provide shelter for the homeless, and jobs for the unemployed. That is as indicative of a grateful person, who does what they can with what they have, as is Jeff Bezos (founder of Amazon.com), who regularly donates hundreds of millions to various worthy causes. All will be remembered not because of their castles or jewels, or skyscrapers or bank accounts, but because what they stood for and stood against catalyzed others to pursue similarly laudable ambitions. Many did, and many more still may.

The most grateful of people have several common characteristics, and three may be the more prominent. First, they are forgiving. Forgiving those who have capriciously, maliciously, willfully, continually, or negatively affected and injured their lives. It is nearly impossible to be grateful and appreciative while one is hateful and vengeful. Secondly, they are compassionate. Compassionate of and for the less fortunate, to those who had neither the mental or physical ability, the circumstances or luck, to be or become what they dreamed they could. Finally, they are appreciative of their good fortune. Whether they "made it" on their own or with the help of others, few make it through life without some luck and some good fortune. Each of these traits is discussed in detail throughout this chapter.

- **Forgiving**. Though few may remember her today, Alice Milliat changed the scope of sports. She felt it incomprehensible that women were not included in the Olympic Games. Way back in 1919, before women even had the right to vote in the United States, she petitioned the Olympic Committee to let women participate in the games (Wood, 2020). Reflective of the times, they refused. It would have been easy for her to walk away disappointed and disillusioned. Instead, she walked away undaunted and undeterred.

She started her own women's sports competition, the International Women's Sports Federation, which created the Women's Olympiad. Enraged by the name, the Olympic Committee demanded she change the name, and in the spirit of cooperation she did. But based on the success of the now-named "Women's World Games," the Olympic Committee capitulated and welcomed women into the Olympic Games (Cooke, 2022). It was not an easy fight for Ms. Milliat, but she persevered not only because of her commitment to her cause and gender, but because she pursued her goal without malice or judgment. She also was willing to forgive those previously against her when they ceased to be.

That is how women entered Olympic sports, and that is why on March 2, 2021, the French Olympic Committee unveiled a statute of Alice Milliat in front of their headquarters in Paris.

Forgiveness may be a lost art, or one that has become increasingly uncommon to see and witness. To some, if not many, we live in offensive and aggrieved times, more against ideas and people rather than for something or someone. Some are more offended by what happened yesterday than what could happen tomorrow, or fighting battles of the past rather than constructing accords in the future. Without exception, we have experienced terrible and unspeakable atrocities at the hands and minds of some toward many. There were truly horrific situations lasting years and decades. Thankfully, though much too late, there came along more enlightened men and women who showed a different path or pursuit.

We should not forget, but we must forgive.

We must forgive if we are to work together, to live together, and to love together. Or, even more simply, if we are to like each other again. It is incredibly difficult to let go of the animosity, bitterness, grudges, sadness, grief, and hatred that has impacted too many. Physical pain may appear the most excruciating to overcome with its more obvious effects, yet it is the mental pain that can paralyze both a person's mind and body.

To forgive the seemingly unforgiveable people who have caused so much harm and pain, whether that was physical or mental, is the mark of a special human being. One person who found the ability to forgive and then became an inspiring figure in history was Pope John Paul II. Here is his story.

• •

Pope John Paul II

He had a bleak childhood. He lost his mother when he was 8 and his father when he was 21. His youth and early years were spent with his country first being occupied by the Nazis and then by the Communists. It was a harrowing period, but during that time he heard the calling to become a priest and thus entered the seminary school (rather than the military). After becoming a priest, he spent the ensuing years encouraging a "spiritual and cultural resistance to the Communist occupation of Poland," a charge he took to Rome when he was elected the first non-Italian cardinal subsequently elected Pope (Saint John Paul II National Shrine, n.d.).

Yet the event that exemplified the basic goodness of Pope John Paul II happened in 1983. In 1981, a Bulgarian man by the name of Mehmet Agca tried to assassinate the Pope. He was shot several times, and upon his arrival at the hospital the Pope was not expected to live. Surprisingly, though near death when first hit by the hail of bullets, some of the Pope's first thoughts were to pray for Mr. Agca. It was also during this time that the Pope sought the spiritual help of the Blessed Mary. The Pope, thankfully, survived.

Then the incredible happened. Two years after the shooting, the Pope asked to meet with Mehmet Agca in his jail cell. He wanted to forgive Mr. Agca for his terrorist actions, and to pray with him so that he could be saved, and his soul redeemed. And so, they met for more than 20 minutes by themselves in that jail cell. It was a message of forgiveness witnessed across the globe.

There is an interesting postscript to this story. More than 30 years after that meeting, and almost 10 years after the death of the Pope, Mehmet Agca visited the Vatican and did the unimaginable: he laid two dozen white roses at the grave of the man he tried to kill all those years before (Burrows, 2014). The power of forgiveness: it betters not only the victim, but the assailant too.

> "we all need to be forgiven by others,
> so we must all be ready to forgive."
> Pope John Paul II
> (Kelly, n.d.)

• •

As we have seen, forgiveness is more about the victim "letting go" than the victim being "let go." It is about the aggrieved no longer being bound by the physical and mental torments of others. It is about focusing less on the pain of history and instead on the promise of the future. Those who have overcome what happened to them, or what happened to those before them, are not subjected to the controls and manipulations of those who follow an unfortunate and unkind path. That is a lesson learned painfully, yet assuredly, by Justice Clarence Thomas.

Supreme Court Justice Clarence Thomas was abandoned by his father and shortly thereafter lost everything in a devasting fire. He lived with his grandfather, who became the most formative influence in his life. He worked hard in school, later graduating from Yale Law School. He persevered through his challenging times and became an imposing figure of the United States Supreme Court. And, like Pope John Paul II before him, Justice Thomas learned to pay no heed to those who continually and constantly demean and degrade his qualifications and accomplishments. He once said:

"you have a number of choices. You could continue to always fight against people who are really distractions. They're people in the cheap seats of life. Or you can do what you went there to do."

Supreme Court Justice Clarence Thomas

Regardless of, or maybe because of, the dismissive and rude behavior some have exhibited toward Justice Thomas, he has now done more in his 30 years on the Supreme Court than many who served before him. When a person needs someone to fight against what is wrong, to work for what is right, Justice Clarence Thomas has always been a reliable vote.

- **Compassionate**. We search far and wide to become part of a community comprised of caring souls; a place where people display sympathy, humanity, sensitivity, and compassion. There are other distinctive characteristics of this type of place, including one of consideration and warmth for all, both the fortunate and the less fortunate. Former college and professional football coach Barry Switzer comes to mind when the subject of compassion is raised. His accomplishments are storied, including being one of only four coaches who have won both a college national championship and a National Football League professional championship (the others being Paul Brown, Jimmy Johnson, and Pete Carroll). That alone cements his legacy, but there is a quote that he is particularly known for.

Coach Switzer had a tremendously hard life. During World War II, his father ran as a bootlegger to raise money, eventually landing in jail because of his choices. It got worse. While home during his senior year in college, his mother shot herself in their home. She had long suffered from depression, and that condition eventually led to her death. She died, sadly, in her son's arms (Hersom, 1986). It got even worse. Just a few short years after that tragedy, his father was murdered in that same home. It was from these experiences that Barry said the infamous quote, "some people are born on third base and go through life thinking they hit a triple" (Boshara, 2018).

Mr. Switzer meant that not everyone has a blessed, idyllic, childhood. Some were born in poverty, violence, neglected, or abandoned. Not all begin on "third base" and instead had to start from home plate, working assiduously to round the bases. And so it began for Barry. Starting at home plate, he worked hard to make it to first base, then second and third, and finally home. And then he tried to round the bases again, and again, and again. Along the way, too, he worked as hard to help those who also started on first base rather than third.

How formative was his childhood? Consider this: the longest job Barry Switzer has ever had was not coaching at the University of Oklahoma or the National Football League, but coaching for the Special Olympics in Oklahoma (News9, 2020). The experiences he had in a harrowing childhood were the exact ones that developed the sense of compassion that made him a good human being. Some good does come from the worst of times, if you learn the lessons.

Compassion is more than sympathy or empathy. It is a genuine concern for those we share this Earth with, even those we may never meet but become aware of their plights and predicaments. But then it is taking action, doing something to intentionally address and conscientiously alleviate the suffering of others. It is an acknowledgment that, like Barry Switzer believed, not everyone begins their journey on third base, and they need some help to round the bases. Thankfully, there are others besides Barry Switzer who have helped those round the bases, and one of those individuals was Mother Teresa, even at only five feet tall, has been an imposing presence in our age.

• •

Mother Teresa

Mother Teresa was incontestably not born on third base, or second or first. She was born of humble beginnings, the daughter of a grocer, but upon her death she not only passed first, second, and third bases, but made many, many trips around the infield in her pursuit to help the poor in India and beyond.

She started as a schoolteacher, but then asked the Catholic Church if she could leave the school and help those beyond the schoolyard. She founded the Missionaries of Charity, a religious congregation dedicated to alleviating the plight of the most destitute and neglected. At its height, her congregation had 4,000 sisters and more than 100,000 volunteers in 123 countries, almost 75% of the world (McGill University, 2007; Wood, 2020).

Eventually, she was awarded many of the prizes given to the greats in recognition of their contributions. She was awarded the Presidential Medal of Freedom by President and Mrs. Reagan, and the Noble Prize, too. In 2016, she was canonized by the Catholic Church as a saint (The Holy See, n.d.). But far and away the greatest reward was the thanks and appreciation she received until her last breath from those she served, the ones who mattered the least to others yet the most to her. By her example, maybe others will learn to care for the often forgotten as much as she did.

"a life not lived for others is not a life"
Mother Teresa

. . . .

The United States has long been a charitable country. For example, from the years 2009 through 2018, the United States led the world in terms of giving and philanthropy. However, it has certainly become a less giving place by some standards. In 2020 the U.S. had fallen to number 19 in terms of giving as a percentage of income, surpassed both by countries in Asia such as Indonesia and Thailand, and countries in Africa such as Ghana, Uganda, and Nigeria (Charities Aid Foundation, 2023; World Population Review, 2023b).

In some ways, it is unfortunate that less is given to charity than in prior years. It may seem representative of a less welcoming place, a less giving place, than in the past. But the U.S. still gives a considerable amount to others, and seems to promote its responsibility to help those who have neither the mental or physical ability to take care of themselves, nor provide for their own welfare. And it is through charity, among several other characteristics, that a sense of community is developed; one where people feel a part of something and want to contribute to something greater. It is a foundational element toward building a place where people want to go, one with hope and charity, giving and benevolence.

- **Good fortune**. We do need to forgive those who harmed us, and to have compassion for those with less than us. There is one more trait that results in a more grateful people, and that is to appreciate the good fortune that has come our way. This is a distinct challenge in the United States and in other lands, mainly because there seems to be more negativity than positivity, more unhappiness than happiness, which consumes too many.

Appreciating one's good fortune centers around attitude and perspective, both trending downward in many surveys and studies in the past years. A 2020 report indicated that more than 80% of U.S. workers suffered from work stress (Carter, 2020) and marriage rates were at an all-time low (Fagan, 2014). We see that younger generations are in school longer and have far less free play. As reported by the General Social Survey, we see that those 18-to-25 years old are developing fewer relationships in 2018 than they did in 1972 (Konrath, 2022). Finally, there was the Harvard-led study published in 2022 which highlighted that in every aspect studied, from happiness to health to meaning to character, those between the ages of 18 to 25, and 26 to 41, rank lower than any other age group (Powell, 2022). The younger are simply more pessimistic and unhappy about their present situations and their prospective opportunities.

No one gets it all, but everyone gets something. The main point is that we must do something with what we have – work to improve something, to advance someone. That is what the famed comedian Jerry Lewis did, and one reason he is remembered today beyond his comedic talents.

. . . .

Jerry Lewis

Jerry Lewis was one of the great comics of his day. He was a television and movie star during the golden age of Hollywood, starring in numerous classics of the day. There was "The Kings of Comedy" and "The Nutty Professor," and who could forget "The Bellboy." His work with Dean Martin lasts to this day as an example of pristine comedic timing and acting brilliance surpassed by few.

But it was his work with the Muscular Dystrophy Association that remains most memorable.

Many, if not most famous people choose a cause to publicize that is close to their heart and home. Think Parkinson's Disease with Michael J. Fox and AIDS with Elizabeth Taylor. Both were admirable choices, but were chosen because their lives were touched by those tragedies. Jerry Lewis stands apart from that trend because he knew no one afflicted with Muscular Dystrophy, yet championed that cause because he thought he could help the less fortunate, those often-younger kids who never really had a chance to do, or be, something. And Jerry Lewis believed they should have that chance.

For 58 years he led the Muscular Dystrophy Association telethon, eventually raising over $2.5 billion for the cause. He received the rewards that come with his generosity – including a special Oscar - but it was the gratitude of "Jerry's

Kids," those he tried to help with Muscular Dystrophy, that meant the most.

"I am probably the most selfish man
you will ever meet in your life.
No one gets the satisfaction or the joy that I get
out of seeing kids realize there is hope."

Jerry Lewis
Associated Press, 2005

• •

Jerry Lewis surely had his adversaries, detractors, and critics. To date, researchers still have not found a cure for Muscular Dystrophy, though advances have been made including the identification of a protein that may restore some muscles of those afflicted with that disease. No matter if the cure has been found, though, Mr. Lewis offered those with that vicious disease the thought that maybe, just maybe, a cure could be found.

He worked tirelessly to promote a cause he had no personal interest in other than to help those who scored lower on the "good fortune" scale. He, like others, understood his obligation and met his responsibility, and he did some good with the time he was afforded on this Earth.

Summary

No matter the place we live or the land we inhabit, there is good in this world if we only choose to look for it. The best of communities, and neighborhoods within them, are composed of individuals and families of many traits and characteristics, from contributing to the general welfare to a graceful disposition. Another of those traits is gratitude. That gratitude manifests itself not only in an appreciation of our good fortune, but in the acknowledgment that we should forgive those who maligned us, and show compassion to those whose choices and circumstances have been unwise or unfortunate.

Gratitude is not inherited at birth. Like attitude or perspective, it is acquired and developed over time. In that regard, the influence of our environment is important, as is luck. We cannot determine who we are born to or under what circumstances we are born in. Some hit the lottery, born to families of wealth and potential, in a land that offers the best of education and professional opportunities, let alone with political and societal stability. Some are not so lucky, and this is where environment becomes so consequential.

Especially at a younger age, the experiences we encounter shape who we are and who we become. Being raised by those with a positive (and sunny) disposition can be the differentiating factor between someone believing they are a victor or a victim, a winner or a loser. They are called the formative years for a reason; they can determine our personality, self-esteem, self-confidence, and character. Surely some personality or self-esteem or self-confidence or character may be acquired or improved upon later, but the lessons learned in the dawn of life often determine the practices we follow until the twilight of life. The hope is that those years are spent within a loving family, among supportive friends, and enclosed in a protective community. That atmosphere is what creates a person of grace and dignity, compassion and understanding, and gratitude and appreciation; all among the best qualities that have been learned from those who came before us, and we can leave to those who come after.

... no one has it all

SUMMARY

When the United States was founded, as with republics in other lands, most people lived within a certain geographical area, had the same occupation, had the same backgrounds and familiar structure, and followed the same religion. There was a degree of commonality among people, making associations and interactions relatively easy and seamless. Though the nature of the times did not lead to a high level of contact between people and communities, there was a lack of communication channels and modes of transportation, nonetheless most could communicate with their neighbors and travel to visit their family and friends.

It was a challenging, somewhat lonely and isolationist existence. In fact, the United States adapted and adhered to an isolationist philosophy for centuries. The country was one of the few that did not engage in foreign battles or try to colonize other foreign lands – they remembered the trauma and disruption that resulted from being colonized themselves. Large towns and cities were not commonplace during these early times either. Not until the advent of technology required that factories and manufacturing plants be constructed to make the new sewing machines and telegraphs which are now demanded by an intrigued public did those exist.

The Industrial Revolution, quite possibly more than any other factor in our history, changed the very nature of the United States. It changed family size and structures, created dozens of work professions, constructed cities of immense size, produced untold wealth among individuals and groups, and saw millions pour into a place where the frontiers and possibilities seemed endless.

It became a different place and advanced in many aspects. Education was at its infancy, human rights became a concern (the Civil War was the first of many battles), and government assumed a more prominent role. As important, were a multitude of people who spoke peculiarly, dressed unusually, and worshipped uniquely. They were different, but also more fun, interesting, compelling, and intriguing to a populace raised in sameness and standardization. The move towards differences, with all its inherent complexities and tremendous opportunities, did not begin at the dawn of the 21st century; it began centuries earlier in the middle of the 19th century.

It didn't work so well.

But the United States' experience was more unique and more complex than any other country in history. Italy, Japan, Nigeria, and Argentina have advantages the United States simply does not have. They all speak the same language, worship the same God, and celebrate the same traditions and customs, to a large degree. They think, believe, and act the same, or at least more similar than more diverse and disparate places like the United States. There are advantages in that aspect: for instance, the Italians and Argentinians have a better understanding, and shared culture, of their neighbors and friends. But there are also disadvantages in that the Japanese and Nigerians may not learn, to an extent, the rich histories, traditions, and customs of those in other lands, including the colors of their dress and the flavors of their food.

A different world.

At the start of this book the statement was made that "we just don't seem to like each other anymore." In retrospect, that is not true. Even with a high degree of familiarity and understanding, we did not associate much with people after the Revolutionary War. Technology, telecommunication, and transportation transformed the way the world lives, transforming a relatively closed community into a more open, freer one, at least in most parts of the world. In that regard, we have entered fortunate times, though in the United States the lack of commonality and uniformity hampers a more understanding and tolerant culture. This is less of a consideration in other nations where a high degree of sameness and conformity represents its people.

It is more difficult in the United States, yes, but more rewarding too, as the presence and prevalence of differences and distinctions create a more colorful, and more dramatic view and experience.

And it really can work.

It has been nearly 250 years, and here we are. Our ancestors were decent in some actions and misguided in others; enlightened in some thoughts, ignorant in others. They did some things terrifically well, and some things tragically bad. Now we must do better. To build a place where we share the most important common values, whatever we believe them to be. Where we compromise our independent thoughts and selfish actions and instead work for the collective benefit of the many. Where we contribute our best to make this place better. Where we are kind and gracious to those we meet, and grateful for whatever good fortune we have been given.

This may not build the perfect country or produce the perfect people. But it does offer the best chance to create a place of decency, and people of honor, that will serve as the model of dignity, civility, hope, and promise for centuries to come.

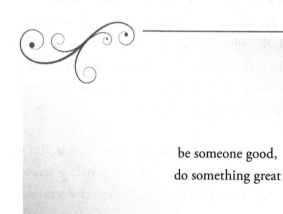

be someone good,
do something great

THE BACKPACK

The search to make a difference—one that defines our existence and determines our legacy—is the seminal journey of our life. It is those who want to make a difference that endures the uncertainties, challenges, and difficulties associated with great change. Through struggles and challenges, the will to make a difference, to make something better for others, overpowers the will to make something better for ourselves. A sense of pride and hope pervades those whose interests far exceed their own, and this ambition can be intoxicating for the individual who comes to believe in the power of a different, yet possibly better, future.

In the dawn of life, we strive to make a living; in the twilight of life, we strive to make a difference. In our younger years, we spend more than we save, use more than we make, and take more than we are given. It is through education, experience, influence, and maturity that our perspectives change as time advances. We realize we may have made a life, but not a difference, and that disappointment and regret haunts our soul. We strive to make a difference because we realize we have not.

If only we would have strived to make a difference throughout the entirety of our life, rather than only at the end when the sands of time slip through the hourglass of time. What if we had worked to save the environment, shelter the homeless, and feed the hungry in our younger years? What if we would have helped those with speech impediments to speak more fluidly or advised high school seniors on how to weather the life-altering experiences as a college freshman? Quite possibly, we could have changed the trajectory of their future rather than waiting until their fate had been determined.

This reminds me of a story I wrote some time ago called *The Story of the Backpack*. I believe that when we are born, we are given a backpack with certain traits, characteristics, talents, and advantages. We then spend the remaining moments of our life perfecting those traits, characteristics, talents, and advantages. We spend our lives trying to "do something" with what we were given in that backpack. It matters little whether we ever achieved our hopes and dreams … what matters is that we tried. We will never have global peace, feed all the world's hungry, or cure catastrophic diseases and illnesses. What matters is that we tried, that we worked to make the world a better place. What matters is that—at the end of our life—you can return the backpack and say that you did the best you could with what you had, that you fought the good fight, that you did what was right, and that—in some small way—your life made a difference in this world.

It is the reason I carry a backpack every day of my life.

...in the end, be able to say
"I did that."

REFERENCES

American Foundation for the Blind. (n.d.) Helen Keller Biography. *American Foundation for the Blind.* https://www.afb.org/about-afb/history/helen-keller/biography-and-chronology/biography

Aratani, L. (2022). Concern as US media hit with wave of layoffs amid rise of disinformation. *The Guardian.* https://www.theguardian.com/media/2022/dec/10/media-layoffs-cnn-buzzfeed-gannett-recount-protocol

Associated Press. (2005, September 12). Emmy honors Jerry Lewis for charity work. *Associated Press: Today Show.* https://www.today.com/popculture/emmy-honors-jerry-lewis-charity-work-wbna9311672

Basker, J. (2018). Frederick Douglass: A life in documents. https://www.gilderlehrman.org/sites/default/files/gli_FrederickDouglass.pdf

Ward, N., & Batalova, J., (2023). Frequently requested statistics on immigrants and immigration in the United States. *Migration Information Source.* https://www.migrationpolicy.org/article/frequently-requested-statistics-immigrants-and-immigration-united-states

Bennett, S. (2023, July 12). Restaurant deliver/takeout statistics 2023 – Everything you need to know. *Webinarcare.* https://webinarcare.com/best-restaurant-delivery-takeout-software/restaurant-delivery-takeout-statistics/

Bhattacharyya, S. (2022). Nordic model: Challenges, characteristics, pros, and cons. *AnalyticSteps.* https://www.analyticssteps.com/blogs/nordic-model-challenges-characteristics-pros-and-cons

Bill of Rights Institute. (2023). George Washington's farewell address. https://billofrightsinstitute.org/primary-sources/washingtons-farewell-address

Biography: Ray Kroc. (2021, April 16). Ray Kroc. *Biography.* https://www.biography.com/business-leaders/ray-kroc

Boshara, R. (2018, April 17). Born on 3rd base? The effects of Head Starts and college on family wealth. *Federal Reserve Bank of St. Louis.* https://www.stlouisfed.org/en/on-the-economy/2018/april/born-third-base-effect-head-starts-college-family-wealth

Bureau of Labor Statistics. (2023, June 22). American time use survey – 2022 results. *Bureau of Labor Statistics: U.S. Department of Labor.* https://www.bls.gov/news.release/pdf/atus.pdf

Bureau of Labor Statistics. (2023b, June 22). Time spent in leisure and sports activities for the civilian population by selected characteristics, averages per day, 2022 annual average. *Bureau of Labor Statistics: U.S. Department of Labor.* https://www.bls.gov/news.release/atus.t11A.htm

Burrows, T. (2014, December 27). Assassin who tried to kill Pope John Paul II puts roses on his tomb…and says he wants to meet Pope Francis. *Daily Mail.* https://www.dailymail.co.uk/news/article-2888550/Man-tried-kill-Pope-John-Paul-II-puts-roses-tomb.html

Cabell, B. (2017, July 4). Are serving clubs dying? *World on the Street.* https://wotsmqt.com/service-clubs-dying/

Cabrera, D. (2021). The whole story of Beethoven's deafness. *California Symphony.* https://www.californiasymphony.org/composer/beethoven/the-whole-story-of-beethovens-deafness/

Calieno, K. (2023). Philippines is among the 'friendliest countries' in Conde Nast Traveller's List. *Proudly Filipino.* https://proudlyfilipino.com/31756/philippines-is-among-the-friendliest-countries-in-conde-nast-travellers-list/

Cambridge Dictionary. (n.d.). Civility. https://dictionary.cambridge.org/us/dictionary/english/civility

Carnegie Corporation of New York. (n.d.). The Gospel of Wealth: The Gospel of Wealth by Andrew Carnegie. *Carnegie Corporation of New York.* *https://www.carnegie.org/about/our-history/gospelofwealth/*

Carter, S. (2020, February 18). The reason older generations are happier than millennials. *Fox Business.* https://www.foxbusiness.com/business-leaders/heres-main-reason-older-generations-are-so-much-happier-than-millennials

Center on Budget and Policy Priorities. (2022, June 9). Policy basics: The supplemental nutrition assistance program (SNAP). *Center on Budget and Policy Priorities.* https://www.cbpp.org/research/food-assistance/the-supplemental-nutrition-assistance-program-snap

Charities Aid Foundation. (2023). World Giving Index 2022: A global view of giving trends. *Charities Aid Foundation.* https://www.cafonline.org/docs/default-source/about-us-research/caf_world_giving_index_2022_210922-final.pdf

Clement, W. (2006). Carrots, sticks and stones. *The Globe and Mail.* https://www.theglobeandmail.com/arts/carrots-sticks-and-stones/article966364/

Clifford, C. (2019). Nearly 68% of the world's richest people are 'self-made,' says new report. *CNBC.* https://www.cnbc.com/2019/09/26/majority-of-the-worlds-richest-people-are-self-made-says-new-report.html

Clifton, J. (2022, September 15). The global rise of unhappiness. *Gallup.* https://news.gallup.com/opinion/gallup/401216/global-rise-unhappiness.aspx

Cohen, L. (2022). Christianity in the U.S. is quickly shrinking and may no longer be the majority religion within just a few decades, research finds. *CBS News.* https://crsreports.congress.gov/product/pdf/IF/IF10501

Conde Nast Traveller. (2022, October 4). The friendliest countries in the world: 2022 readers' choice awards. *Conde Nast Traveller.* https://www.cntraveller.com/gallery/friendliest-countries-world

Cooke, R. (2022, August 19). How Alice Milliat brought women into the Olympics. *RTE: Ireland's National Public Service Media.* https://www.rte.ie/brainstorm/2022/0819/1316517-alice-milliat-womens-sport-olympics-1922/

Coombs, L. (2023). Lessons learned: Judge not – there, but for the grace of God, go I. *Laurie Coombs.* https://lauriecoombs.org/2013/03/14/lessons-learned-judge-not-there-but-for-the-grace-of-god-go-i/

Cost, B. (2021, July 27). Americans have fewer friends than ever before: study. *New York Post.* https://nypost.com/2021/07/27/americans-have-fewer-friends-than-ever-before-study/

Crossway. (2022). 10 key Bible verses on grace. *Crossway.* https://www.crossway.org/articles/10-key-bible-verses-on-grace/

Dermody, K. C. (2023, January 1). 16 countries with the world's friendliest people. *Travel Inspiration.* https://www.tripstodiscover.com/16-countries-with-the-worlds-friendliest-people/

Desilver, D. (2023, April 18). Who pays, and doesn't pay, federal income taxes in the U.S.? *Pew Research Center: Research Topics.* https://www.pewresearch.org/short-reads/2023/04/18/who-pays-and-doesnt-pay-federal-income-taxes-in-the-us/

Dickinson, S. (2022, July 12). Glasgow has been named the world's friendliest city. *TimeOut*. https://www.timeout.com/news/glasgow-has-been-named-the-worlds-friendliest-city-071222

DuBois, W. E. B. (1903). *The talented tenth*. Yale MacMillan Center: Gilder Lehrman Center for the Study of Slavery, Resistance and Abolition. https://glc.yale.edu/talented-tenth-excerpts

Dunlop, J. (2021). 30 most influential entrepreneurs of all time. *Income*. https://www.incomediary.com/30-most-influential-entrepreneurs-of-all-time-2/

Encyclopedia Britannica. (2023, June 23). Helen Keller: American author and educator. *Encyclopedia Britannica*. https://www.britannica.com/biography/Helen-Keller

Fagan, A. (2014). Why adults are less happy than they used to be. *Psychology Today*. https://www.psychologytoday.com/us/blog/our-changing-culture/201511/why-adults-are-less-happy-they-used-be

Flynn, J. (2018, February 22). Fraternal disorder: As moose lodges struggle for relevance, an internal battle engulfs Folsom chapter. *Sacramento News and Review Archives*. https://www.newsreview.com/sacramento/content/fraternal-disorder-as-moose-lodges-struggle-for-relevance-an-internal-battle-engulfs-folsom-chapter/25897447/

Forbes. (2023, Jan 25). Unemployment is low, but so is the labor force participation rate – What's going on in the U.S. Labor Market? *Forbes*. https://www.forbes.com/sites/qai/2023/01/25/unemployment-is-low-but-so-is-the-labor-force-participation-rate---whats-going-on-in-the-us-labor-market/?sh=2d0d03da244e

Frederick Douglass Heritage. (2023). *Quotes*. http://www.frederick-douglass-heritage.org/quotes/

Freetheslaves. (n.d.). Slavery in history. *Free the Slaves.* https://freetheslaves.net/slavery-today-2/slavery-in-history/

Gatto, L. (2018, June 16). Stefan Edberg thinks sportsmanship award should be renamed after Federer. *Tennis World.* https://www.tennisworldusa.org/tennis/news/Roger_Federer/56326/stefan-edberg-thinks-sportmanship-award-should-be-renamed-after-federer/

Glen. (2013, September 17). The stick is the law. And so is the carrot. *Christ the Truth.* https://www.christthetruth.net/2013/09/17/the-stick-is-the-law-and-so-is-the-carrot/

Hall, L. (2022, February 24). 54 uplifting confidence quotes to boost your mind. *Country Living.* https://www.countryliving.com/life/inspirational-stories/a39116740/confidence-quotes/

Hanson, M. (2022, June 15). U.S. public education spending statistics. *Education Data Initiative.* https://educationdata.org/public-education-spending-statistics

Harper, J. (2020). Broadcast coverage of Trump 95% negative, according to new study. *The Washington Times.* https://www.washingtontimes.com/news/2020/aug/17/broadcast-coverage-of-trump-95-negative-according-/

Hersom, B. (1986, August 3). On tape, Switzer remembers rugged upbringing. *The Oklahoman.* https://www.oklahoman.com/story/news/1986/08/03/on-tape-switzer-remembers-rugged-upbringing/62719028007/

Hill, F. (2020, November 5). Public service and the federal government. *Brookings.* https://www.brookings.edu/policy2020/votervital/public-service-and-the-federal-government/

Himber, V. (2022, October 20). Employer-sponsored health insurance statistics: What the data tell us. *eHealth*. https://www.ehealthinsurance. com/resources/small-business/how-many-americans-get-health-insurance-from-their-employer

History. (n.d.). Gorbachev resigns as president of the USSR. *History.com*. https://www.history.com/this-day-in-history/gorbachev-resigns-as-president-of-the-ussr

Holcomb, J. (2022, August 11). What is grace? Bible definition and Christian quotes. *Christianity.com*. https://www.christianity.com/wiki/christian-terms/what-is-grace.html

House Budget Committee. (2023, April 5). Budget staff working papers: A growing culture of government dependency. *House Budget Committee*. https://budget.house.gov/press-release/budget-staff-working-papers-a-growing-culture-of-government-dependency/

Human Rights Career. (n.d.). 10 root causes of racism. *Human Rights Careers*. https://www.humanrightscareers.com/issues/root-causes-of-racism/

Hussein, M., & Haddah, M. (2021). Infographic: US military presence around the world. *Aljazeera*. https://www.aljazeera.com/news/2021/9/10/infographic-us-military-presence-around-the-world-interactive

Internal Revenue Service. (2023a). Historical highlights of the IRS. *Internal Revenue Service*. https://www.irs.gov/newsroom/historical-highlights-of-the-irs

Internal Revenue Service. (2023b). SOI tax stats – IRS data book. *Internal Revenue Service*. https://www.irs.gov/statistics/soi-tax-stats-irs-data-book

Jones, J. (2021). U.S. church membership falls below majority for first time. *Gallup.* https://news.gallup.com/poll/341963/church-membership-falls-below-majority-first-time.aspx

Jones, J. (2022). Confidence in U.S. institutions down; average at new low. *Gallup.* https://news.gallup.com/poll/394283/confidence-institutions-down-average-new-low.aspx

Keller, H. (1934, September). Going back to school: The true meaning of the value of education. *Home Magazine.* https://www.afb.org/HelenKellerArchive?a=d&d=A-HK02-B225-F02-029.1.1&srpos=4&e=-------en-20--1--txt--%22use+his+brains%22------3-7-6-5-3--------------0-1

Kelly, E. (n.d.) Pope John Paul II and his message of forgiveness. *Loyola Press.* https://www.loyolapress.com/catholic-resources/scripture-and-tradition/church-leadership/pope-john-paul-ii-and-his-message-of-forgiveness/

Kenton, W. (2020, November 22). What is the Organization for Economic Co-Operation and Development (OECD). *Investopedia.* https://www.investopedia.com/terms/o/oecd.asp

Kenton-2, W. (2021, January 27). Nordic model: Comparing the economic system to the U.S. *Investopedia.* https://www.investopedia.com/terms/n/nordic-model.asp

Klein, E. (2020). *Why we're polarized.* Simon & Schuster.

Konrath, S. (2022, October 21). The younger generation isn't lazy; they're burned out. *Greater Good Magazine: Science-based insights for a meaningful life.* https://greatergood.berkeley.edu/article/item/the_younger_generation_isnt_lazy_theyre_burned_out

Kratz, J. (2021). Madam C. J. Walker's rags-to-riches story found in the holdings of the National Archives. *National Archives*. https://prologue.blogs.archives.gov/2021/07/22/madam-c-j-walkers-rags-to-riches-story-found-in-the-holdings-of-the-national-archives/

LaMotte, S. 2020, January 23). Cremation has replaced traditional burials in popularity in America and people are getting creative with those ashes. *CNN Health*. https://www.cnn.com/2020/01/22/health/cremation-trends-wellness/index.html

Laslo, M. (2020, January 20). The New York Times presidential endorsement shows why newspapers must end the practice. *NBC News*. https://www.nbcnews.com/think/opinion/new-york-times-presidential-endorsement-shows-why-newspapers-must-end-ncna1118796

Lemelson-MIT. (n.d.) Johann Gutenberg: Movable type printing press. *Massachusetts Institute of Technology*. https://lemelson.mit.edu/resources/johann-gutenberg

Library of Congress (n.d.). Manuscript/mixed material: Image 4 of Thomas Jefferson to Charles Yancey, January 6, 1816. *Library of Congress*. https://www.loc.gov/resource/mtj1.048_0731_0734/?sp=4&st=text

Lyrics on Demand. (n.d.) Cheers theme lyrics: Where everybody knows your name, lyrics by Gary Portnoy and Judy Hart Angelo. *Lyrics on Demand*. https://www.lyricsondemand.com/tvthemes/cheerslyrics.html

Martins, Ryan. (2020, July 9). Why 'your truth' is anything but. *Connecticut's Nonprofit Journalism*. https://ctmirror.org/2020/07/09/why-your-truth-is-anything-but/

McBride, A. (2021, May 27). The evolution of voting rights in America. *National Constitution Center*. https://constitutioncenter.org/blog/the-evolution-of-voting-rights-in-america

McCain, A. (2023, May 21). 22 McDonald's Statistics (2023): Restaurant counts, facts, and trends. *Zippia: The Career Expert.* https://www.zippia.com/advice/mcdonalds-statistics/

McDonald, M. (n.d.). National turnout rates: 1789-present. *United States Election Project.* https://www.electproject.org/national-1789-present

McGill University. (2007). Mother Teresa. *McGill University.* https://www.cs.mcgill.ca/~rwest/wikispeedia/wpcd/wp/m/Mother_Teresa.htm

McWhinney, J. (2022). The Nordic model: Pros and cons. *Investopedia.* https://www.investopedia.com/articles/investing/100714/nordic-model-pros-and-cons.asp

Meares, H. (2020, November 6). "Whatever I did, I did": The obstinate life of Bette Davis. *Vanity Fair.* https://www.vanityfair.com/hollywood2020/11/bette-davis-autobiography-feud

Medicare Advocacy. (2022). Medicare enrollment numbers. *Center for Medicare Advocacy.* https://medicareadvocacy.org/medicare-enrollment-numbers/

Memmott, M. (2012, June 27). Sign of peace: Queen Elizabeth shakes hand of former IRA commander. *National Public Radio.* https://www.npr.org/sections/thetwo-way/2012/06/27/155828020/sign-of-peace-queen-elizabeth-shakes-hand-of-former-ira-commander

Michals, D. (2015). Harriet Tubman. *National Women's History Museum.* https://www.womenshistory.org/education-resources/biographies/harriet-tubman

Monticello. (n.d.). If a law is unjust... (spurious quotation). *The Jefferson Monticello.* https://www.monticello.org/research-education/thomas-jefferson-encyclopedia/if-law-unjustspurious-quotation/

Moore, J. (2003). Booker T. Washington, W. E. B. Du Bois, and the struggle for racial uplift. *Rowman and Littlefield.* https://rowman.com/ISBN/9780842029957/Booker-T.-Washington-W.E.B.-Du-Bois-and-the-Struggle-for-Racial-Uplift

Movies Staff. (2022, September 22). Bette Davis vs. Warner Brothers. https://moviestvnetwork.com/stories/bette-davis-vs-warner-brothers

Nadler, J., & Schulman, M. (2006, August). Civility. *Markkula Center for Applied Ethics at Santa Clara University.* https://www.scu.edu/government-ethics/resources/what-is-government-ethics/civility/

Nash, J. (2023, June 8). Full-time and part-time employment: A deeper look. *VettaFi Advisor Perspectives.* https://www.advisorperspectives.com/dshort/updates/2023/06/08/full-time-and-part-time-employment-a-deeper-look

National Archives. (n.d.). Observing Constitution Day. *National Archives: Educator Resources.* https://www.archives.gov/education/lessons/constitution-day/ratification.html

National Constitutional Center. (2023, June 21). The day the Constitution was ratified. *National Constitution Center.* https://constitutioncenter.org/blog/the-day-the-constitution-was-ratified

National Cremation. (n.d.) Why is cremation becoming more popular in the US? *National Cremation.* https://www.nationalcremation.com/cremation-information/why-is-cremation-becoming-more-popular-in-the-us

National Museum of American History. (n.d.). Germans in the Midwest. *National Museum of American History: Behring Center.* https://americanhistory.si.edu/many-voices-exhibition/

peopling-expanding-nation-1776%E2%80%931900/pushed-and-pulled-european-immigration-0

National Park Service. (n.d.). A man of many firsts: George Washington's first inauguration. *National Park Service: Article.* https://www.nps.gov/articles/000/george-washington-inauguration.htm

NCES. (2022). Back-to-school statistics. *Institute of Education Sciences: National Center for Educational Statistics – United States Department of Education.* https://nces.ed.gov/fastfacts/display.asp?id=372

News9. 2020, December 10). Barry Switzer's legacy centered on compassion. *News9.* https://www.news9.com/story/5fd2bc55e35e120bc9ed03dd/barry-switzers-legacy-centered-on-compassion

nsn2020 (2020, July 29). Elks sees slight increase in national membership. *Nonprofit Sector News.* https://nonprofitsectornews.org/2020/07/29/elks-sees-slight-increase-in-national-membership/

NTUF. (2022). Government spending in historical context. *National Taxpayers Union Foundation.* https://www.ntu.org/foundation/tax-page/government-spending-in-historical-context

Oliver, H. (2022, July 11). The 53 best cities in the world in 2022. *TimeOut.* https://www.timeout.com/things-to-do/best-cities-in-the-world

Olya, G. (2023). Here's how much retirees actually have in savings (Hint: it's not enough). *Yahoo.* https://www.yahoo.com/now/much-retirees-actually-savings-hint-160009167.html

Owen, J. (2023, May 16). The world's friendliest countries – as chosen by you. *Rough Guides.* https://www.roughguides.com/articles/worlds-friendliest-countries-voted-by-you/

Perry, M. (2020). Tribute to Margaret Thatcher. *American Enterprise Institute.* https://www.aei.org/carpe-diem/tribute-to-margaret-thatcher/

Pew Research Center. (2022). Modeling the future of religion in America. *Pew Research Center.* https://www.pewresearch.org/religion/2022/09/13/modeling-the-future-of-religion-in-america/

Powell, A. (2022, September 15). Why are young people so miserable. *The Harvard Gazette.* https://news.harvard.edu/gazette/story/2022/09/why-are-young-people-so-miserable/

Providence Forum. (n.d.). The rules of civility and decent behaviour in company and conversation. *Providence Forum.* https://providenceforum.org/story/rules-civility-decent-behaviour-company-conversation/

Putnam, R., & Campbell, D. (2010). American grace: How religion divides and unites us. *Social Capital Project.* https://www.pewresearch.org/religion/2010/12/16/american-grace-how-religion-divides-and-unites-us/

Rakitov, S. (n.d.) Ray Kroc. https://codepen.io/prosperousrf/details/NNvNRX

Rappeport, A. (2021, April 13). Tax cheats cost the U.S. $1 trillion per year, I.R.S chief says. *The New York Times.* https://www.nytimes.com/2021/04/13/business/irs-tax-gap.html

Reed, B. (1999, July 1). Willie Whitelaw dies aged 81. *The Guardian.* https://www.theguardian.com/politics/1999/jul/01/uk.politicalnews6

Research, Statistics and Policy Analysis. (2023, April). Monthly statistical snapshot. *Social Security.* https://www.ssa.gov/policy/docs/quickfacts/stat_snapshot/

Saint John Paul II National Shrine. (n.d.). About: Saint John Paul II. *Saint John Paul II National Shrine.* https://www.jp2shrine.org/en/about/jp2bio.html

Schweikert, D. (2019, December 18). The space between: Renewing the American tradition of civil society. *United States Congress: Joint Economic Committee.* https://www.jec.senate.gov/public/index.cfm/republicans/analysis?ID=78A35E07-4C86-44A2-8480-BE0DB8CB104E

Small Business Labs. (2022). Tracking and forecasting the trends and shifts impacting the future of work, small business, and the Gig economy. *Small business Labs.* https://www.smallbizlabs.com/2022/12/the-number-of-us-independent-workers-continued-to-surge-in-2022.html

Sorvino, C. (2014, July 8). The Gilded Age family that gave it all away: The Carnegies. *Forbes.* https://www.forbes.com/sites/chloesorvino/2014/07/08/whats-become-of-them-the-carnegie-family/?sh=5b97d0dd7b55

Spellen. S. (2022, June 8). Booker T. Washington, the Tuskegee Institute and New York City. *Spellen of Troy. https://suzannespellen.substack.com/p/booker-t-washington-the-tuskegee*

Stanford University. (n.d.). Gandhi, Mohandas K. *Stanford: The Martin Luther King, Jr. Research and Education Institute.* https://kinginstitute.stanford.edu/encyclopedia/gandhi-mohandas-k

Statista. (2023a). College enrollment in the United States from 1965 to 2020 and projections up to 2030 for public and private colleges. *Statista.* https://www.statista.com/statistics/183995/us-college-enrollment-and-projections-in-public-and-private-institutions/

Statista. (2023b). Share of households in the United States that paid no individual income tax in 2022, by income level. *Statista.*

https://www.statista.com/statistics/242138/percentages-of-us-households-that-pay-no-income-tax-by-income-level/

Sunde-Brown, D. (2021, November 10). Why Portugal is the friendliest country in the world. *The Real World.* https://www.trafalgar.com/real-word/portugal-friendliest-country-in-the-world/

Talbott, S. (2022, March 9). The man who lost an empire. *Brookings.* https://www.brookings.edu/articles/the-man-who-lost-an-empire/

The Holy See. (n.d.) Mother Teresa of Calcutta (1910-1997. *The Holy See: Vatican.* https://www.vatican.va/news_services/liturgy/saints/ns_lit_doc_20031019_madre-teresa_en.html

Trading Economics. (2023a) United States government spending to GDP 2022 data - 2023 forecast. *Trading Economics.* https://tradingeconomics.com/united-states/government-spending-to-gdp

Trading Economics. (2023b) United States employment rate. *Trading Economics.* https://tradingeconomics.com/united-states/employment-rate

Trading Economics. (2023, July). United States – Public spending on education, total (% of GDP). *Trading Economics.* https://tradingeconomics.com/united-states/public-spending-on-education-total-percent-of-gdp-wb-data.html

Tuskegee University. (n.d.). Dr. Booker Taliaferro Washington: Founder and first president of Tuskegee Normal and Industrial Institute. *Tuskegee University: TU Presidents.* https://www.tuskegee.edu/discover-tu/tu-presidents/booker-t-washington

U.S. News and World Report. (2022, September 27). These are the friendliest countries. *U.S. News and World Report.* https://www.usnews.com/news/best-countries/rankings/friendly

United States Congress Joint Economic Committee. (2019). Losing our minds: Brain drain across the United States. *United States Congress.* https://www.jec.senate.gov/public/index.cfm/republicans/analysis?ID=78A35E07-4C86-44A2-8480-BE0DB8CB104E

United States Congress Joint Economic Committee. (2019). The space between renewing the American tradition of civil society. *United States Congress.* https://www.jec.senate.gov/public/index.cfm/republicans/analysis?ID=78A35E07-4C86-44A2-8480-BE0DB8CB104E

United States Department of Commerce. (1944). Population: Estimates of labor force, employment, and unemployment in the United States, 1940 and 1930. *United States Department of Commerce, Bureau of the Census.* https://www2.census.gov/library/publications/decennial/1940/population-labor-force/population-labor-force.pdf

University of Maryland. (2018, October). Where are America's volunteers? A look at America's widespread decline in volunteering in cities and states. *University of Maryland: School of Public Policy.* https://dogood.umd.edu/sites/default/files/2019-07/Where%20Are%20Americas%20Volunteers_Research%20Brief%20_Nov%202018.pdf

University of Virginia. (1817). Thomas Jefferson on politics and government: Educating the people. *University of Virginia.* http://jti.lib.virginia.edu/jefferson/quotations/jeff1350.htm

Urban, W., & Wagoner, J. (2004). *American education: A history.* Routledge: Taylor & Francis Group.

Vile, J. R. (2020, April 3). So help me God. *The First Amendment Encyclopedia.* https://www.mtsu.edu/first-amendment/article/1718/so-help-me-god

Vocabulary.com. (n.d.). Civility. https://www.vocabulary.com/dictionary/civility

Walker, M. & Matsa, K. (2021, September 20). News consumption across social media in 2021. *Pew Research Center.* https://www. pewresearch.org/journalism/2021/09/20/news-consumption-across-social-media-in-2021/

Washington, G. (1796). Farewell address. *Mount Vernon.* https:// www.mountvernon.org/george-washington/religion/religious -freedom/

Watson, M. (2023, August 3). Opinion column: Primary election day – your vote matters." *Michael Watson: Secretary of State for the State of Mississippi, Press Releases and Columns. https://www.sos.gov/press/ opinion-column-primary-election-day-your-vote-matters*

Wimbledon. (2018, February 23). Are players right to cry and defy Kipling at Wimbledon. *Wimbledon: Tennis News & Articles.* https:// wp.wimbledondebentureholders.com/2018/02/23/tears-better-stiff-upper-lip-wimbledon/

Wood, S. (2020, November 8). 50 famous women that made an impact on history. *HistoryColored.* https://historycolored.com/ articles/5790/50-famous-women-that-made-an-impact-on-history/

World Population Review. (2023). Immigration by country 2023. *World Population Review.* https://worldpopulationreview.com/country-rankings/ immigration-by-country

World Population Review. (2023b). Most charitable countries 2023. *World Population Review.* https://worldpopulationreview.com/country-rankings/ most-charitable-countries

York, E. (2023, January 26). Summary of the latest federal income tax data, 2023 update. *Tax Foundation.* https://taxfoundation.org/publications/ latest-federal-income-tax-data/

Zane, M. (2023, Jan 30). What is the working age population in the U.S. [2023]: Statistics on prime working age population in America. *Zippia: The Career Expert*. https://www.zippia.com/advice/working-age-population/

Zumbrum, J. (2022, September 16). Some monarchies endure, but monarchies are in decline. *The Wall Street Journal*. https://www.wsj.com/articles/some-monarchs-endure-but-monarchies-are-in-decline-11663320634?ns=prod/accounts-wsj

I did my best,
now you do better

Printed in the United States
by Baker & Taylor Publisher Services

Printed in the United States
By Bookmasters